Copyright

Muscle Memory and Imagery: Better Tennis
First edition

Title ID: 7636099
ISBN-13: 978-1978025752

BISAC: Sports & Recreation / Tennis

Editor: Bill Smith

Printed by CreateSpace

Readers are advised to consult with, and get approval, from a physician and other qualified health professional before participating in sport, especially tennis. Further, there should be frequent followup regarding advise to continue, or not, related to playing or practicing tennis, especially as related to Muscle Memory Practice. Author does not take any responsibility for any possible consequences related to the above.

Serious effort was taken to ensure the accuracy of the material herein, but there are no guarantees related to this. Final responsibility is solely the responsibility of the reader

No warranties of any kind are expressed or implied. Readers acknowledge that the author is not engaging in the rendering of legal, financial, medical or professional advice.

By reading this document, the reader agrees that under no circumstances am I responsible for any injuries, losses, damages, etc. that may occur as the result of the use of information contained within this document, including, but not limited inaccuracies, errors, omissions, or just being wrong related to my theories, proposal, suggestions, etc.

Sorry all the legalese. It seems necessary in today's world. Nevertheless, I want you to know that I would be flattered if you wanted to use sections of my book. Just contact me via the "Contact" section on my web site "mmitennis.com".

Dedication and Acknowledgements

First and foremost, I want to thank my wonderful family for enabling my tennis indulgences. I have the best family in the world!

Next I want to thank my tennis buddy Sven for his friendship, creating the Sven simulator, and letting me use it my book. I also have enjoyed the heck out of our Indian Wells trips!

Then there is Bill Smith, another tennis buddy and friend. He patiently put a lot of time and energy into editing my book. Great job. Thanks!

Then, of course, there is Brendan, my tennis pro and friend. There could not be a better pro and all around great person!

I am blessed to have so very many guys and gals as tennis friends. However, if I listed everyone's name and what they mean to me, then this book would be much longer. Words cannot really express my appreciation! So I guess I will have to go with a simple but sincere thanks. Love you all! You make it all fun and worthwhile.

I also want to thank all the pro women and men players! You provide endless inspiration and fascination. Thanks so much!

I especially want to thank Roger Federer, the GOAT of all sports. It is not just the physical ability and prowess, but it the way you carry yourself, and the kindness and respect that you give to everyone else.

Finally I want to express thanks to Larry Ellison for making Indian Wells the great tournament that it is! I just love it!

Contents

Section I: Introduction to All Muscle Memory

Prologue

Origins of New Tennis Theory

The Prelude to Epiphany –
Understand the Sequence of Events
that Brought about Muscle Memory Theory,
The "Perfect Storm" that
Brought about this Evolutionary Leap Forward.

The Prologue explains the Catalyst!

I was bored. Yea . . . that's about it.

This project started one summer a while back. I began thinking about why we do not get better at tennis. At the time, I had played very little through the summer. The Texas heat is brutal, so why suffer. My game, especially my forehand, was off. I was losing rallies. Of course, what would one expect after not playing much? Nevertheless, I started thinking about the bigger issue of why we only progress to a certain point, and not much beyond that.

We all take lessons at times. Some months, I hit against the ball machine regularly, really about 3 times a month – rarely twice per week. Then for at least a couple of times a year, I go over 2 to 3 months without using the ball machine at all. Another friend goes to clinics every week. Another takes lessons regularly. Although I guess our games have improved over the last few years, we really have not gotten much better. Why – and how does one get better? Surely there must be a better way to improve your game – a way toward "Better Tennis"!?!?

If no mistake have you made, yet losing you are
a different game you should play
Yoda

So I reviewed the medical and Internet literature about the subject. There is not much there. To me, the way we hit is primarily due to muscle memory. In thinking about this, a focus on muscle memory seemed to be the most useful approach.

Being of scientific mind and training, I felt there should be "Laws". Certainly in physics there are principles or laws, such as $E=mc^2$, $F=ma$, etc. Biologic systems also have laws – Starling's law of the heart, formulas for cardiac output and renal function, etc. But there were no laws, or anything else close to it, that I could find for muscle memory.

So I thought I should make some up. I mean why the heck not? I was bored. I had the time (not much tennis in the hot Texas summer). Plus I was getting kind of interested in all this. I made up

"Laws of Muscle Memory" based on common sense, my knowledge and experience with biological systems, and my thorough reviews of the literature on multiple topics related to muscle memory and tennis.

Good laws should be very clean and simple statements of facts. Of course, the practical application of the laws to your tennis game, and getting results, would be more difficult. I worked on this and sort of liked the results. Some of my thoughts and conclusions go back to what I had learned from lessons, personal experience, and my time spent on the ball machine.

In the past, most of my ball machine workouts consisted of what I call the "Clinic Workout" – A round or two of forehands, then backhands, then volleys, and by that time 45 to 90 minutes had passed. After that I usually played better the next 1 to 2 outings. Overall, it was an enjoyable workout, being a good exercise, making me physically tired, and resulting in mild short-term improvement. I also enjoyed the peace and quiet of being alone and not having to think or talk. Let's face it, at work or home, there is always something going on requiring your attention and interaction. The time on the tennis court exercising alone by hitting balls from the ball machine is very relaxing.

During some other ball machine workouts, I would work on only one or two shots, instead of the clinic workout. Usually, this was directly due to the frustration of a day where a particular shot was really off. At other times, I only hit one shot because I just felt like hitting a particular shot for no reason at all. As I thought back, I realized that after I had these sessions, I seemed to improve more and it seemed longer lasting than with the clinic workout.

There were two times I had done this that stand out. The first was with my forehand. Brendan, my tennis pro friend, convinced me to hit with the new modern grip. I was awful at first. To compensate, I spent about two months hitting nothing but forehands. Now my forehand is my best shot.

Also, several years ago, my volleys were my worst shot – well below average. I spent a couple of months practicing primarily on volley ball machine workouts. This was before I had developed my "Muscle Memory Theory". I used the ball machine about 3 to 4 times per month for two months – hitting nothing but volleys. After that, my volleys were the best they had ever been, and it stayed with me ever since. Even now, the volleys have never gone back to my previously awful state.

So considering these experiences and my extensive review of muscle memory literature, I made my "Laws of Muscle Memory" and applied the laws to specifically learn how to improve one's tennis game. I tried to adhere strictly to the Laws of Muscle Memory, along with a healthy dose of common sense. I also applied my knowledge of neuroplasticity and neurobiological systems. I like the results.

I do not usually comment much about what I've done in the past, but actually, I have a lot of awards and honors. At one time, I was Medical Director of Rehabilitation Hospital. I won a National Award as Medical Director and was selected to be on the National Physician's Advisory board. As directors, we would fly someplace and meet about 2 to 3 times per year. This was quite unusual, in that I am in Internal Medicine and Geriatrics and everyone else was specialized in Rehabilitation, Neurology, and/or Sports Medicine. All were prominent in their field.

I made several friends and I sent one of them my thoughts on muscle memory. He liked it and sent it to his siblings. One is a coach who has coached a Heisman trophy finalist, a major league baseball player, a state golf champion, etc. His sister has opened multiple learning centers. They liked it and were complimentary. I feel I have had some learned reviewers who were supportive. I felt encouraged. So I wrote some more and explored other topics. This book is the result of that endeavor.

Hence the purpose of this book is to pass along the Laws of Muscle Memory and its application to your tennis – in hopes of Better Tennis. This is all basically a theory (or group of theories), but it has proved true in my own experience. It is also based on scientific research and evidence.

So the theory may be good but what about results? The only way to see if there is validity or truth to a theory is to test it. The theory briefly says you need to hit a specified stroke for 45 to 90 minutes 3 to 4 times per week (4 is better) for 3 weeks. Sounds simple enough, but really, there is a bit more to it than that. To really appreciate it, you will have to read the theory, and then put in time and effort to test it all out. Less would work some, but not as well. If you follow through with the Muscle Memory Practice, then in theory, your game will significantly and noticeably improve for many months or years (at least so the theory says).

I also added sections on personal observations that help me, as well as a section on statistical probability and the importance of this. I then became interested in Imagery, so I included my review on this potentially useful topic. Also, since my theory involves extra practice and work, I summarized a chapter on "How to Accomplish Muscle Memory Practice".

Taken as a whole, this all will involve fundamentally changing (at least somewhat) how your very concept of tennis should be practiced, but I believe it will move you toward "Better Tennis".

> *"Some people play tennis all their lives*
> *but never get better.*
> *Those people are not willing to take a fresh look*
> *at what they do or to consider changing it.*
> *Good players recognize that getting better often*
> *means making an investment in new approaches.*
> *For a while they may get worse as they wrestle*
> *with new and unfamiliar techniques,*
> *but eventually they surpass their old plateau.*
> *The new techniques offer more long-term potential"*
> Roger Fisher and William L. Ury
> (1991, p. 212)

Chapter 1: Laws of Muscle Memory

Muscle memory is what determines your strokes and makes your tennis game what it is – for the good or for the bad.

I propose the following laws of muscle memory. By understanding these laws, you can apply them to your training and your tennis game. You will become a better player.

Laws of Muscle Memory

1. **Your tennis strokes are due to muscle memory.**
2. **Muscle memory is the result of permanent changes in the brain, nerves, and muscles.**
3. **Permanent changes occur through repetition in a concentrated period of time.**
4. **Repetition by doing it right in practice is how you hit good strokes during a match.**
5. **Learning different patterns back to back may cause forgetting of the initial one.**
6. **Once your muscle memory is in place it "forgets" slowly, if at all.**
7. **The temporary improvement that occurs during practice or matches should not be considered learning, but rather a transient performance effect.**

Notes

- Law #7 is from Wikipedia ("Motor learning", 2017, para #1).
- Forget the hyperbole that starts the Prologue. I was just trying to contrast the "I was bored" statement, and add a little humor.

Chapter 2: Application of Training to Your Tennis Game
Laws 1-4

Law #1 – Your tennis strokes are due to muscle memory.

Muscle memory "involves consolidating a specific motor task into memory through repetition. When a movement is repeated over time, a long-term muscle memory is created for that task, eventually allowing it to be performed without conscious effort. This process decreases the need for attention and creates maximum efficiency within the motor and memory systems" ("Muscle Memory", 2017, para 1).

Another definition would be "performing a motor action without conscious effort".

Law #2 – Muscle memory is the result of permanent changes in the brain, nerves, and muscles.

Your muscles "memorize" due to changes in the neural circuitry involving the brain, nerves, and muscles. This causes you to do it "that way" during a match. Technically, this is called "procedural memory".

Procedural memory (also called implicit memory) is memory for how to do things. It is not based on the conscious recall of information. "Procedural memory is primarily employed in learning motor skills...It is revealed when one does better in a given task due only to repetition – no new explicit memories have been formed, but one is unconsciously accessing aspects of those previous experiences" ("Memory", 2017, under heading "Procedural"). Think of it like riding a bicycle. After you learn it, you don't have to remember any steps, you just do it.

"Procedural memory guides the processes we perform and most frequently resides below the level of conscious awareness. When needed, procedural memories are automatically retrieved and utilized for the execution of the integrated procedures involved in both cognitive and motor skills...Procedural memories are accessed and used without the need for conscious control or attention...Procedural memory is a type of implicit memory (unconscious memory) and long-term memory...Procedural memory is created through 'procedural learning' or, repeating a complex activity over and over again until all of the relevant neural systems work together to automatically produce the activity. Implicit procedural learning is essential to the development of any motor skill or cognitive activity" ("Procedural memory", 2017, para. #2, #1, #3).

"At a cellular level, motor learning manifests itself in the neurons of the motor cortex. Using single-cell recording techniques, Dr. Emilio Bizzi and his collaborators have shown the behavior of certain cells, known as 'memory cells', can undergo lasting alteration with practice. Motor learning is also accomplished on the musculoskeletal level. Each motor neuron in the body innervates one or more muscle cells, and together these cells form what is known as a motor unit.

For a person to perform even the simplest motor task, the activity of thousands of these motor units must be coordinated. It appears that the body handles this challenge by organizing motor units into modules of units whose activity is correlated". ("Motor learning", 2017, under heading titled "Physiological approach")

Law #3 – Permanent changes occur through repetition in a concentrated period of time.

I define repetition over a concentrated period of time, as it applies to tennis strokes, as 45-90 minute sessions 3 to 4 times per week over a 3-week period. The practice time needs to be concentrated because the passage of time quickly erodes the neurochemical processes. Any skill obtained during a practice session is lost within 2 to 3 days if not reinforced. Furthermore, the practice time needs to last at least 3 weeks (optimally) for permanent changes to occur related to muscle memory. For one example, 3 weeks is the usual time period for inpatient rehabilitation after a significant stroke or cerebral accident. That is, this is the minimal time period for new connections and skills to be really learned.

Law #4 – Repetition by doing it right is how you hit good strokes during a match

In order to train yourself to hit good strokes, the ones that win points, most of the practice strokes you hit must be good. Forget about immediate results. Repeatedly hitting good strokes is the way to get results that matter – the ones that make for a winning difference in your matches. The ones that stay with you over time. Good strokes are the result of muscle memory developed by doing it properly over and over again until the permanent changes occur. You first must acquire the skill (the acquisition phase), and then develop, master, and retain the skill by much repetition in a concentrated period of time so it can be retrieved without conscious effort during match play (the consolidation phase). Simply put, the way you practice is the way you play.

More on Laws #3 and #4

Tennis drills usually consist of hitting a bunch of forehands, then backhands, then volleys, and so on. Rarely does one work on only one stroke (for example, a cross-court forehand) for the entire drill, or even the majority of the time spent on a lesson.

But let's say this does happen. You and your pro are going to have a practice on the cross-court forehand. Even then, if you only practice the cross-court forehand (and not the forehand down the line), about all that happens is that 250 forehand cross-courts are hit, if that many. To generalize, this means about 25 are hit poorly as you warm up. The next 200 are hit in a mediocre fashion (the "so-so stroke" that you usually hit and want to improve – like you do in a match), and then finally 25 are hit well because you have "found the groove". Now players and pros tend to think – "you know what to do" – "you have it down". Sounds like an excellent lesson for the cross-court forehand. You are hitting it well and have improved. Then, since you are hitting well on the cross-court forehand, you switch to the backhand, and maybe repeat the same cycle, then onto the volleys, etc. Note that this is more than most go through, as most of the time I see students switching before they found the groove.

But what have you really done? What have you "trained" your muscle memory to do? The result is that you have trained your motor memory to hit poorly, or reinforced your mediocre "so-so" stroke 90% of the time. Do the math – 225 strokes hitting poor to mediocre shots, and 25 strokes hitting good shots. Little wonder that one's game improves slowly, if at all. Little wonder you end up hitting like you always do when you play the match the next day, and then wonder why your game is off because you were hitting so well yesterday at the end of the lesson.

So do you want to take your game to a permanent higher level? To do so, you must build muscle memory. Go back to the end of your practice session, the part where you are now hitting well. Now you must consolidate this so it becomes permanent. To accomplish this, you must hit an additional 500 balls after you start hitting well – all cross-court forehands (actually 2000-5000 balls, or more, would be preferable – but use the 500 number). You now have greater than a 66% chance of hitting better, rather than a 10% chance.

Simply put, the more the repetition of hitting well, the more likely that permanent changes develop that will keep you hitting well, especially when you need it. You are training yourself to play better during a match because most of your time and practice is spent training your muscle memory to hit the "better than usual" forehand. You are acquiring the skill by temporary performance improvement. Now, because you keep hitting it well, you are more likely to retain the skill because you are laying down neural circuitry and motor pathways. You are creating muscle motor memory for good strokes – better than your usual stroke, and it is becoming permanent. It makes sense. The more you hit well, the more probable that you will hit it well at a later point in time.

But the goal is to permanently elevate your game to the next level. This cannot occur in only one, two, or even three, sessions.

It takes time for the brain to become re-formed (re-programmed) so that the better stroke remains (and becomes the preferred pathway, rather than your usual mediocre stroke) for long-term retention. You will need to practice that one shot – say the cross-court forehand – at this rate for 45 to 90 minutes, 3 to 4 times per week (again, 4 is better), for consecutive weeks. From a technical perspective, it takes 3 weeks (the optimum) for synapses to generate, for cellular chemical factories and receptors to be up-regulated and down-regulated, and for nerve and motor endings to undergo structural change. It takes this long for layers of myelin to be laid down in a meaningful fashion.

Here are three common sense examples that further serve to illustrate this.

- Let's say you want to work out with weights and get stronger. You go in with a trainer and have a 1½ hour workout. You then walk out of the gym brimming with confidence that now you are stronger, and stronger forever, because of the single workout. Obviously, this would be self-delusional thinking and wrong. The only way to get stronger is to have the same workout 3 to 4 times a week over several weeks. Why would the muscle memory involved in developing an improved stroke be any different? Why would you realistically think that a single good workout session with a pro is going to have any meaningful improvement on your game? The answer is obviously it will not. Muscle memory involved in hitting a good stroke is more complex than strengthening of the muscles. To really improve your game, you need permanent change in the brain, nerves, and muscles (Muscle Memory Law #2). Muscle memory becomes permanent by repetition in a concentrated period of time (Law #3). Repetition by doing it right is how you hit good strokes during a match (Law #4).

- A good metaphor for establishing muscle memory is to think of it as trying to walk across and over a large marshy field and dense forest interlaced with swamps and dense underbrush. What you want to do first is to make a path so future trips will be easy. In order to get from point A to point B, you first have to figure out the best route across. However, once you figure out the best route, there still is no path. In order to make a path across the field and swamps you have to go over the route several times over a period of a few weeks. The more often you go over the route in a short period of time, and the more times you repeat that exact route, the more quickly and more permanent the path will come into existence. (Once per week will not establish a path). Establishing neural paths and muscle memory is the same.
- Let's say you want to run a 10 K race. Obviously, training once per week is not going to do it. You can hire a personal trainer and he/she can tell you all the right things to do, but not much happens till you "do it" – that is run/train (in tennis – practice your chosen stroke) 3 to 4 times per week for a few weeks.

However, note one importance difference in my theory vs running, etc. In running, the training effect will stay with you only for a few weeks, but per muscle memory theory, if you work 3 to 4 times per week (I emphasize, 4 is best) for 3 weeks on only one shot – then the muscle memory stays with you, meaning your ability to reliably make that shot stays with you. If true, that would be awesome, and have tremendous implications related to tennis.

Note another practice implication, and this is one that goes exactly opposite the way things are usually done. Suppose you go out and are hitting one particular shot really well that day in practice, or in a match. We all have experienced this – who knows why, but it is a fact. But what often happens when you then decide to practice more? Most likely, you do not hit the shot that you are hitting really well – instead you work on the rest of your game. This is something you can change for the better. Consider it a rule – "Always keep hitting after you are hitting well".

What you really need to do, in order to improve your overall game for the long term, is to keep hitting that shot over and over – the one that seems to be going well. Take advantage of the fact that it is going exceptionally well. Spend time reinforcing all the pathways and neuromuscular changes that are occurring at that time. Hit nothing but this shot for an extended period – hopefully the 3 weeks. Prolong being in the zone and perfect the excellence. Remember, as per the laws of muscle memory – the more you hit the shot, the more permanently ingrained that shot (whether you hit it well or poorly) will become, and the more likely it will become a permanent part of your game.

Notes

- I believe Monica Seles used Muscle Memory Practice. You may remember that she was the victim of a horrible knife attack when she was only 20 years of age. Her career was never the same after that. What you may not remember is how tremendously successfully she was. Prior to that, Seles was "the youngest ever French Open champion at the age of 16. She went on to win eight Grand Slam singles titles before her 20th birthday and was the year-end world number 1 in 1991 and 1992". ("Monica Seles", 2017, para #2). So how did she train to achieve that remarkable degree of success? Nick Bollettieri writes in his book, "She would practice a single shot for a week, two weeks, three weeks – whatever it took to master it" (Bollettieri, 2001, p. 207). Sounds like Muscle Memory Practice to me!

Chapter 3: Muscle Memory Practice

Repetition in a Concentrated Time

Muscle Memory Practice is repetition in a concentrated period of time, with no further type of practice involved. It especially means no further practice after your practice session on that one stroke. It is dedicated, focused practice. The concept of Muscle Memory Practice builds on deliberate practice (also called "Deep Practice" by Daniel Coyle of "The Talent Code"). So let me summarize some of the principles of "Deliberate Practice", then state the key elements of Muscle Memory Practice.

It is not how much you practice,
it is how you practice
(A paraphrase of a Jimmy Conners quote – Bollettieri, 2001, p. 206)

Deliberate Practice . . .

- Requires focus on detecting and correcting your mistakes for progress – to specifically target your mistakes. This means it must be highly structured. This contributes mightily to mastering your mistakes.
- Requires challenging yourself – it stretches you – you must push the edge of what you can do – strive for what you cannot consistently perform. You must practice the skill at a more challenging level.
- Requires revisions – You must search for methods to improve performance. Strive so that with each repetition you learn more. This process is enhanced if you have a pro or a knowledgeable friend to give immediate feedback to refine your efforts.
- Requires repetition – a LOT of repetition – but it cannot be mindless repetition – it must be focused, deliberate repetition (thus called Deliberate Practice).

Muscle Memory Practice . . .

- Requires deliberate practice.
- Requires singular focused practice of one type on only one specific skill (for example, a cross-court forehand).
- Requires that the repetition is in a concentrated period of time (daily, or at least every other day, practice extending at least 3 weeks).
- Requires that no other types of practice occupy your practice session (as back-to-back practice of different strokes will likely cause forgetting of the initial one). It is especially important to avoid practicing any other type of stroke at the end of your practice session, even a casual "hitting around".

"I fear not the man who has practiced 10,000 kicks once,
but I fear the man who has practiced one kick 10,000 times"
Bruce Lee

Additionally, you "Slow It Down" to learn technique and consistency. My Muscle Memory Theory says you do focused practice on only one aspect of your game. Do this for 3 weeks every other day (though every day would be the ideal). You do not perform any motor skills activity or other types of athletic practice. You especially do not do any other motor skill activity after a practice session for that day. This relatively brief effort will improve your game "forever" (or a really long time). Note also that technique, consistency, and repetition are of prime importance. In later chapters, I will go into why slowing it down is of prime importance to obtaining proper technique and consistency. Forming muscle memory is best accomplished by starting slowly to exactly reproduce the motor skill activity. Then much repetition.

These quotes reinforce the validity and effectiveness of Muscle Memory Practice:

"Practice begins when you get it right"
Kimberly Meier-Sims
(as quoted by Daniel Coyle, 2012, p. 55)

"One of the most fulfilling moments of a practice session
is when you have your first perfect rep.
This is not the finish—it's the new starting line
for perfecting the skill until it becomes automatic"
(Daniel Coyle, 2012, p. 55)

"Arguably the most famous violin teacher of all time, Ivan Galamian,
made the point that budding maestros do not engage in deliberate practice spontaneously:
If we analyze the development of the well-known artists,
we see that in almost every case
the success of their entire career was dependent on the quality of their practicing"
(Ericsson, Prietula, & Cokely, 2007, under section titled: Find Coaches and Mentors)

Practice doesn't make perfect but perfect practice really helps.
Anonymous

"The way to be successful is to learn how to do things right,
and then do them the same way every time"
Pat Riley
(Mike Klinzing 2015, para. 3)

As noted above, it takes time for the brain to become re-formed (re-programmed) to where the better stroke remains and becomes the preferred pathway, rather than your usual mediocre stroke. That requires 45 to 90 minutes, 3 to 4 times/week, for 3 consecutive weeks.

So how does this go in real life? From personal experience, in the first session it was hard to hit 10 in a row. In session 2 and 3 and 4, you will hit in the 10 to 20 range. Yes – it will be boring – expect it to be boring. As you practice, you may feel you are not making progress – it may feel like you have stalled out. But hang in there. Stay with the dedicated, focused problem-solving "deliberate practice" sessions. Stay with the Muscle Memory Practice. Then, on session 5 to 6, expect it to start improving. Expect to go 5 to 6 sessions before it really "clicks". It will click! Then keep hitting the same shot, even though you are hitting it better than you ever have. Burn it into your muscle memory!

Don't practice until you hit it right
Practice until you can't hit it wrong!
Unknown

Remember, to establish Muscle Memory, you are trying ramp up, build, and make permanent the brain/muscle/neuron neurochemical factory connections, etc., that create the muscle memory. This is a dynamic process. The base for the improvement starts going away quickly, actually beginning in the 24 to 48 hour period after your practice. When you practice just once, there is little muscle memory to build on after just 2 days, and probably none after 3 days (I describe this in further detail at the end of Chapter 4). Brain chemistry is a very dynamic process, essentially building and deconstructing all the time. Short term memory (acquisition) erodes quickly. It becomes long term memory (muscle memory) by frequent repetition in a concentrated period of time.

More personal experience – I hit nothing but backhands one March. The practice sessions did not go as smoothly (in terms of getting 3 to 4 practices per week) as I had hoped, but it was closer than anything that I had done before. Twice over that month, I had a series of connected, dedicated practices against the ball machine, hitting only backhands. The first one was 5 times in 7 days. The second was 5 times in a 10-day period. Unfortunately, the period between the two sessions was separated by over one week. I could definitely tell that I lost ground. However, I did start hitting my backhand the best I ever had. I even took a lesson from my pro friend, Brendan, after my first group of 5 sessions in a 7-day period. He said that I was hitting my backhand the best ever. I also won my division in the main Austin tournament – The Courtyard Classic! (I won at age 64, and I had never ever won a tournament before).

I also had another interesting observation. My forehand stroke was also clearly improved, although I had not even come close to practicing it – not even part of a single ball machine round. I think it was because I had started really focusing on the basics – the fundamentals (described later in the book). I was "Getting Set" faster. I was doing a "Head Turn" – that is, watching the ball. I was focusing on, and therefore hitting, the "Sweet Spot" of the racket better (for more on this, see the chapter on "Transference").

As noted above, my game fell off when I did not have a focused, dedicated practice for one week. Since then, I have experimented with different time spans. I have concluded that **there is a fall off if you go a full two days without practicing your dedicated shot.** This is again analogous to the weight lifting analogy. That is, you lose a lot of ground if you only work out twice per week. It takes 3 to 4 sessions per week, preferably 4, to maintain, reinforce and importantly – to improve!

It follows that it is better to hit 4 times in one week, rather than once per week for one month. To practice once per week is not likely to meaningfully improve your game due to the Laws of Muscle Memory, any more that lifting weights once per week will make you all Arnold Schwarzenegger-like.

Therefore, if you are attempting a 3-week period of dedicated Muscle Memory Practice, it is important to try to get on the court and practice at least every other day. However, it is no big deal if, once or twice in a three week period, you go two days in a row without practicing. As the old saying goes:

Do not let the perfect be the enemy of the good
Voltaire
("Perfect is the enemy of the good", 2017, para. 1)

This means it is more important to get a lot of practice sessions in the 3-week time span than it is to never attempt it because you might not be able to practice every other day.

Another tip: Keeping a log reinforces your learning related to Muscle Memory Practice! Record the data and review it: Keeping a journal can be very helpful when you are trying to improve in any field. By tracking your progress, you can see if you are moving ahead or not. You should figure out the effectiveness of your learning methods and strategies. Your written entries, including your personal observations and analysis, are important. What works and what doesn't? Track and learn from them! Your log should be a treasure chest of helpful, insightful information.

Notes

- There is experimental evidence to support my theory, something beyond my own personal experience. Kleim, Hogg, VandenBerg, Cooper, Bruneau, & Remple (2004) document that motor skills do not develop uniformly across training sessions. In their experiment, they noted that trained animals obtained motor skills in a reaching task by day 3, and significant improvements continued to occur after 3 and 7 days of training. However, significant increases within the motor cortex was not detectable until after 10 days of training (meaning although the skills were improved, detectable changes within the brain itself did not occur until daily training sessions reached day 10). To me, it lends great support to the concept that it will take at least that many sessions (in a relatively short period of time) for meaningful structural changes to occur – that is for muscle memory to develop (in the above experiment, the structural changes were an observable increase in synapse number). Another group of researchers state, "changes in map topography that endure beyond the training session are not detectable until after 10 days of training" (Kleim, et al, 2004, p. 632). This shows if you want the improvements in your training to be long lasting, then it will take a minimum of 10 days for that task. (Note that 10 times of every other day equals about 3 weeks – again, this is the initial minimal time needed to make observable changes in the brain, changes that will therefore be long lasting).

- A bit more detail from Kleim, et al. He noted that after 3 days of training, performance improved from 18% to 39%; after 7 days, it improved from 23% to 52%; and after 10 days, accuracy improved from 21% to 61%. Again, the measurable changes in the brain (the motor cortex) did not occur until day 10, and this was an increase in the number of synapses per neuron. The "reorganization in response to motor training requires more than one week. It is possible that during the initial training experience, changes in movement representation occur, but do not persist outside of the training period" (Kleim 2004, p. 632 – I added the underlines for emphasis). Therefore, significant brain changes are only evident in the later phases of motor skill acquisition.
- The above Deliberate Practice compilation is from different sources – Ericsson, Visser, Wikipedia, ("Practice (learning method)", 2017), Coyle, & Colvin. It was hard to find definitive line-item, clear, brief and simple definitions describing Deliberate Practice – specifically, the principles/steps/characteristics/methods, etc., that relate to my theories. In fact, I never found a single source that smoothly tied into Muscle Memory Practice. Deliberate Practice characteristics varied from 4 essential elements to 11, depending on the source. Therefore, I did a compilation from what I considered the best sources. I summarized a few essential points that seemed most relevant to Muscle Memory Practice.
- Reading and learning about Deliberate Practice is well worth your time. In my review, I drew primarily from the three authors. First, K. Anders Ericsson is the primary author and researcher of "Deliberate Practice". He deserves a Nobel Prize in my opinion. Also, the Deliberate Practice concept is discussed in wonderful fashion in the books "The Talent Code" by Daniel Coyle, and "Talent is Overrated" by Geoff Colvin. Both these books are on my "Highly Recommended" list at the back of this book, as is Ericsson's landmark article.
- I reviewed other sources for this book. It is impressive how often the recommendation for "buying a notebook" occurred. This is because they felt it was important. So... "Keep a log!" It is repeatedly recommended. Some examples:
  - Per Daniel Coyle, "A high percentage of top performers keep some form of daily performance journal. Serena Williams uses notebooks...What matters is not the precise form. What matters is that you write stuff down and reflect on it. Results from today. Ideas for tomorrow. Goals for next week. A notebook works like a map: It creates clarity" (Coyle 2012, p. 19).
  - Even Nick Bollettieri says to do this. To quote from his book – THE VERY FIRST PAGE of the entire book – "Throughout more than four decades of coaching, I have interacted with people from all walks of life. I continue to be disappointed with myself for not having kept a daily diary, something to bolster my memory and prevent the inevitable loss of detail that accompanies the passage of time. So before you end up with the same regrets, start keeping a diary today. Diaries become treasures that recall the minutia of an event, those details that make it worth remembering in the first place" (Bollettieri, 2001, xi – the first page of the Preface).
- The paraphrase of the Jimmy Conners quote stems from the original quote: "It's not the quantity but the quality that counts" (Bollettieri, 2001, p. 206).

Chapter 4: Even More on Laws #3 and #4
Acquisition and Consolidation

Law #3 – Permanent changes occur through repetition in a concentrated period of time.

Law #4 – Repetition by doing it right in practice is how you hit good strokes during a match.

This is a technical chapter. I apologize if it seems too academic. However, I consider it essential to your understanding of how the learning of new motor skills occurs, that is, how muscle memory develops. Also, the science involved explains the components and structure of Muscle Memory Practice. It gives the basis for why Muscle Memory Practice should be the most effective, efficient way to Better Tennis in the shortest period of time.

First, a brief general discussion of acquisition and consolidation. Acquisition is the process of first mastering the skill. It is learning within a session, or perhaps 2 to 3 sessions. It is short term. It fades in just a few short days. Consolidation is when you develop, master, and retain the skill by much repetition in a concentrated period of time. The result is that the motor skill (your "good" and much improved tennis stroke) is retrieved without conscious effort during match play. Consolidation is a slow phase of learning developed over many training sessions – days to weeks. This is how long-term permanent changes will occur and ultimately persist. The parts of the brain that control new learning are different from the parts that control movements that have already been learned/acquired. Reworded, the learning of new motor skills, or muscle memory circuits, involves different areas of the brain than skill areas previously mastered. All of this is the complicated process of consolidation. It is long term memory. It is muscle memory.

Now, what follows are the facts: Bullet points from academic experiments and studies. In fact, it is referenced just like it would be in a journal. This is the hard, raw science that supports my theories. If this does not appeal to you, then you can skip to the section immediately below the bullet points.

Acquisition

- In acquisition, motor skill learning is characterized by an initial fast phase. There are rapid improvements in performance that can be observed within a single training session, and across the first few sessions (Kleim, Hogg, VandenBerg, Cooper, Bruneau, & Remple, 2004).
- Within a single learning session, your learning peaks, or plateaus, then starts to fall off. If you go too long, learning is diminished. You get sloppy. Technically, this is called Habituation. (See notes at the end of the chapter for further comments on Habituation).

Consolidation

- The progression to long term memory is referred to as consolidation (Shadmehr and Brashers-Krug, 1997).

- "Memory consolidation refers to a process whereby a memory becomes increasingly resistant to interference from competing or disrupting factors with the continued passage of time" (McGaugh study as cited in Walker, Brakefield, Hobson, & Stickgold, 2003 – p. 616).

- In consolidation, motor skill learning is characterized by a slow phase of learning. This incremental progression of learning occurs across multiple training sessions (Kleim, Hogg, VandenBerg, Cooper, Bruneau, & Remple, 2004).

- The learning of a motor skill continues and is enhanced after the practice has ended, but it takes several hours (optimally an overnight sleep) before this occurs. Walker, Brakefield, Morgan, Hobson & Stickgold reported, "Following practice of a specific motor sequence, delayed performance improvements only occur across a night of sleep, while waking periods of 4, 8 or even 12 hours offer no such performance enhancements" (as quoted in Walker, Brakefield, Hobson, & Stickgold, 2003, p. 617).

- Sleep is critical to improving memory – to stabilizing the memory and converting it from a short-term memory to a long-term memory: That is consolidation (Rasch, & Born, 2013). Simply put: Sleep = enhancement. Sleep consolidates motor memory and leads to better performance. Rephrased, sleep improves performance.

- The brain changes. These changes are specific to the motor cortex for the skill that has been practiced. One study documents that by week 4 of training "the extent of cortex activated by the practiced sequence enlarged compared with the unpracticed sequence" (Karni, Meyer, Jezzard, Adams, Turner, & Ungerleider, 1995, p. 155).

A few facts about both acquisition and consolidation

- As early acquisition fades, consolidation strengthens (Shadmehr and Brashers-Krug (1997). Acquisition is short-term memory. This fades completely and relatively quickly. But acquisition is not totally lost if it is reinforced (other training sessions) close to the previous session (within 1-2 days) and repeated. With this kind of repetition, the brain transforms the short-term memory (acquisition) into long term memory (consolidation). Acquisition and consolidation are two totally separate mechanisms working within the brain. However, even though they are separate, they are both essential, sequential components of how muscle memory works. They are functionally dependent, completely complementary, but totally different.

- "Complex motor tasks require several training sessions interspersed with periods of rest and sleep. For these tasks, acquisition and consolidation are interlocked, forming a complex sequence of events" (Luft, & Buitrago, 2005, p. 214).

- The learning that occurs during acquisition and consolidation involves different regions and pathways within the brain, and this changes as it phases from acquisition to consolidation. Different regions and pathways learn at different rates ("Motor Skill Consolidation", "Muscle Memory", "Declarative Learning", "Procedural Memory", 2017).

Here is a different way of saying all that:

The regions and paths of the brain that control our current motor skills are different from those that are involved in learning new motor skills (Luft & Buitrago, 2005). The processes involved are also different. The learning of new motor skills, or muscle memory circuits, involves different areas of the brain than skills already mastered.

The learning curve

The neuromuscular connections, visual connections, proprioception, muscle movements, balance, coordination, and other components of a good tennis stroke are completely different. They are all controlled by different parts of the brain and body that "learn" at different rates. The brain coordinates visual, motor, proprioception, muscle movement, balance, coordination, etc., to make muscle memory work. This is especially true for the consolidation phase. This is where the long term permanent changes will occur and ultimately persist. Below is my own proposed learning curve. I have seen different learning curves, but they only would show smaller bits and pieces, and not "the big picture" as is shown here. This composite is what I propose. (Some may call it speculative, heresy, conjectural, theoretical – whatever – nevertheless, I like it and it has a lot of science to back it up.)

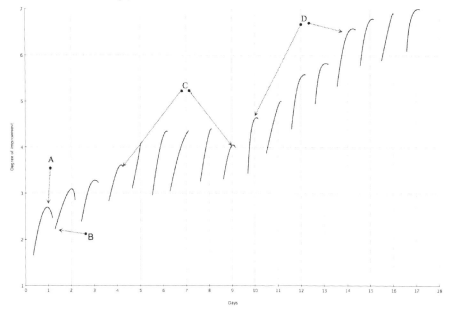

Reference point A: This is acquisition – improved performance in a single training session in one day. Note that the performance peaks and then falls off. That is, continued effort worsens your performance skill. The single day learning curve part of my proposed graph shows that during a long daily performance, your improvement stops, and then actually declines. This is due to "Habituation". Your motor skills are getting worse. There is diminishing response (that is, the learning/perfection of your tennis stroke) to a repeated stimulus (the tennis ball coming at you). Your body/brain is losing focus. Think of it as sensory overload.

You can only learn so much in a single session. If you persist beyond that, you begin to have diminishing returns. You would actually be "messing up" what you had accomplished. Fatigue also can contribute to poor habits and faulty learning. So do not overdo it on any single day (you also risk overuse injury). No amount of work in the beginning can fix it all. To have permanent improvement, it takes time. It is just like cement being set: It takes time. It is just like growing a plant – you can water and fertilizer it twice a day and you may be good in the long run; however, it still takes time. That is just how it is.

For purposes of my proposed graph, I imagine (and made the graph to illustrate) that during the first two practice sessions, the tennis player practices too much. The lines on day 1 and 2 show the "Degree of Improvement" peaks, then falls off. After day 2, I presume the player now knows to stop before practice begins to deteriorate (due to habituation and maybe fatigue). The player has learned to stop before the degree of improvement actually starts to regress, to decline (you would be losing the improvement that you have gained). I know it is hard to determine when this occurs. You will need to figure that out with your individual practice. It is prudent that you try and stop each practice before you decline. It is extremely important that your last practice be your best, as that is what is most likely to be consolidated into long-term muscle memory.

Now observe what happens from one day to the next. You have a good practice session and hit nothing but cross-court forehands. Generally, the next day (reference point B), you are not as good as you were at the end of the preceding day. You may not do things as well, but you still most likely are doing it better than at the beginning of the previous day's practice. So now it is the next day. With practice, you get back to your previous level of play, and you progress more quickly than you had the previous day. Then, with more practice that day, you will improve further, beyond the previous level (this is a generalized statement – meaning it is true most of the time, but not all of the time).

If you think about it, the same pattern is common to both musicians and dancers. This should especially strike a chord (I know – poor pun) if you ever took music lessons. Musicians usually practice daily. They improve when they practice. The next day they are not as good as when they had quit the previous day, but they get there as they practice further. If you have had music lessons, then you know how you improve with daily practice (not once per week) when focused on a few select pieces of music. Then, as the practice continues, the musician gets even better, until finally the piece is learned. I am not sure why this model of improved motor performance via muscle memory is used so commonly in music and dance, but not applied to sports such as tennis. For some reason, it is accepted and expected in tennis (and other sports), that if you practice once or twice a week, you will improve. This would be a ridiculous supposition in dance or music. Draw your own conclusions about how logical it would be to apply to tennis.

Note also, IMPORTANTLY, the lowest level of performance after several days of practice is better than the peak performance in the first 1 to 2 sessions.

One other biological fact: You do not learn at a fixed additional amount every day, so do not expect this. The body does not learn in fixed intervals. Learning is too complex. This is especially true of complex motor movements related to tennis. Instead, learning occurs in irregular, inconsistent increments – meaning some days there is only a little progression, and some days there is a lot. Overall, it is an irregular, but nevertheless positive upward progression.

The specifics will vary from one player to another, but there are generalities. Note on the graph there is a relatively slow, almost flat learning level for sessions for 4 to 9 (reference point C). This is a Transition period. We resist in that we want to do our preferred – our old already learned pattern. So we go through a period of instability. So do not be surprised if you stall out after the first few sessions.

But if you persist, then eventually you adopt preferred new patterns. There is clear improvement on days 10 to 14 – you then can execute the improved strokes that you want to hit consistently (reference point D).

More biological facts: There is a physiological reason for this. A tennis stroke is a complex movement. There are many different elements that go toward the development of a good stroke. Multiple muscles, nerves, and proteins are changing; protein synthesis is occurring; myelin is forming; new synapses are forming; receptors are shifting up and down, etc. – many, many changes are happening within your body. Different body systems (muscles, nerves, brain, etc.) ARE different, and "learn" at different rates. "Because motor learning is made up of a number of distinct processes…, they consolidate with different time courses and at different anatomical locations" (Krakauer & Shadmehr, 2006, p. 62). The way they learn is also different. Different parts of the brain are different, and therefore internalize the new skills at different rates. Different parts of a stroke are being consolidated (completed), some more quickly than others. Sometimes it may even be an entirely different mechanism of learning. The more complex the movement, the more the body must learn, especially with a movement as complex as a tennis stroke.

To facilitate learning of new motor skills, or refinement of existing motor movements, the brain/body breaks segments of the movement into smaller parts. Motor skill learning occurs in stages. Some scholars refer to this as "chunking". Muscle memory is your body learning by dividing the movement into "chunks". This forms the neurobiological basis for learning. Chunks are formed at irregular intervals because your body learns them at different rates – which implies that a complex sequence of tasks will not work smoothly together until all the links in the chain are connected well. As noted, one body system will pick up the new skill at a rate faster (or slower) than another. For example, the balance component of your improved stroke may "learn" more slowly than the "spatial recognition" component, and both learn differently than the "muscle" (strength) component that is needed to complete the stroke. In fact, the overall stroke may worsen until the "balance" part of the stroke gets its act together and catches up with the muscle and spatial components. However, when completed, these chunks are then put together to form the entire movement.

Chunking is the accumulation of small, discrete circuits. Science provides evidence that this is how we learn our motor skills ("Chunking (psychology)", 2017). Our tennis strokes are made of chunks – parts of physical movements learned by the body separately, then added to other learned chunks – all finally making up the entire stroke. The brain, nerves, muscles then combine all this together – visually seeing the ball, getting set, proprioception (see below), calculations related to the speed spin direction of the incoming ball, etc., into your (hopefully) smooth, well-coordinated movement that makes an excellent tennis stroke – just the way Federer does it! Federer's strokes are great because he has repeated the movements (the chunks) often enough that he knows how to perform it all as one fluid, precise, beautiful movement. When he fires to hit a passing shot, he doesn't have to think.

Again, dancers and musicians do this routinely by practicing only sections of their performance, and then when the parts are mastered, they meld them together to perform the entire piece. The analogy also applies directly to tennis – think Federer, who has been described as the Baryshnikov of tennis (Google Roger Federer as Baryshnikov).

Therefore, it may take several sessions before you hit a "Click" moment (see below, next chapter). As noted previously, when you are learning a new movement, different aspects are learned at different rates. The Click will occur when all the aspects begin to be consolidated.

Do not forget that established muscle memory is the result of permanent changes (see Law # 2 – "Muscle memory is the result of permanent changes in the brain, nerves, and muscles"). Again, different body organ systems are "learning", but what they are actually doing is building and establishing the framework for permanent connections, that is the permanent pathways of muscle memory (laying down myelin, forming synaptic connections and networks, etc.) that encode the final muscle memory. This does take time. This is why consolidation takes time. This also explains why the final stroke is a complex "final product". The complexity of the stroke determines how long the chunks take to meld together.

In summary, within a good single practice, a player improves over the practice session. This is acquisition, also known as transient performance improvement. While helpful, this does not improve your game over the long term. Long-term muscle memory occurs over several sessions in a concentrated period to time. For long-term improvement, it is subsequent learning over time (consolidation) that is establishing motor memory. This takes several days to a few weeks (in a concentrated period of time) because one learning session builds on the previous learning session. Also, for consolidation to occur, periods of rest, as in overnight sleeping, are necessary.

I am not sure I can emphasize the importance of continued hitting after you are hitting it well, at least if you really want to continue for the long term at your higher level of skill (meaning improved shots – faster, deeper, more accurate, more consistent, hit at better angles, etc.). There will be great temptation to move to another stroke, but that would be negating much of your previous efforts and practices. You would simply and quickly lose the higher level of skill that you just obtained. Joiner and Smith (2008, p. 2949) note, "after reaching a high level of performance during an initial training period, additional training that has little effect on performance can lead to substantial improvements in long-term retention", and "the greater the degree of overbearing, the greater the retention of the task". Other researchers note that after practice ceases, the neural connections return to previous levels, but if there is subsequent training, these connections are stabilized and endure for long periods (Xu, Yu, Perlik, Tobin, Zweig, Tennant, Jones, & Zuo, 2009). Joiner and Smith (2008, p. 2949) also note that "the slower learning process contributes to long-term retention". So show some self-discipline – keep practicing for several sessions (the more the better) after you are hitting it well!

Notes

- Sleep is needed for long-term changes to occur. So a good night's sleep, or even a nap, is needed for, and contributes to, improved tennis strokes and games (pretty cool for those of us who like to take naps).

- Proprioception refers to the body's ability to sense movement and position within joints, muscles, hands, arms, shoulders, legs, etc. This is how we know where the parts of our bodies are – their positioning in space and relative to other body parts, the angle that we are holding our rackets, etc. We do not have to look. We sense where they are. It gives us the feedback that we rely on for complex sporting movements, such as a tennis stroke. It is important in all everyday movements but especially so in complicated sporting movements, where precise coordination is essential.
- There is something almost magical about the time period of 3 weeks in the true learning (consolidation) of a new motor task. This is corroborated across multiple studies. I need to emphasize this is the theoretical gold standard. Shorter time sequences (say 4 to 5 Muscle Memory Practice sessions in one week) also improve your game! But recognize, the longer the sequence of closely-related practice sessions, the better and more permanent the result.
- Great coaches were intuitively aware of the critical importance of teaching in chunks. Daniel Coyle (author of "The Talent Code") notes one of John Wooden's key coaching techniques: "He taught in chunks, using what he called the 'whole-part method' – he would teach players an entire move, then break it down to work on its elemental actions" (Coyle, 2009, p. 114).
- Habituation is a decreased response or performance when repeatedly doing the same task. A more formal definition is that habituation is the decrease of a response to a repeated eliciting stimulus that is not due to sensory adaption or motor fatigue. ("Habituation", 2017, para. 1). The occurrence of Habituation affects the acquisition phase. Your learning peaks, then diminishes. You actually get worse. Therefore, if you practice too much during a single session, it can have negative effects. Note also from Ericsson, Krampe, & Tesch-Römer (1993) – "Deliberate practice is an effortful activity that can be sustained only for a limited time" (p. 369). To go beyond the time you are fully focused and concentrated on your deliberate practice is probably detrimental.
- Most sources felt that sleep is needed for consolidation to occur, but one study did note improvement beginning at 8 hours. However, they also reaffirm that more than 8 hours works better: "large improvements occurred thereafter" (Karni & Sagi, 1993, p. 250).
- If you are more interested in neuroplasticity (the way the brain learns new skills), search Wikipedia on "Hebbian theory". Briefly it proposes an explanation for the adaptation of neurons in the brain during the learning process, describing a basic mechanism for synaptic plasticity ("Hebbian Theory", 2017). Also, if interested, review "Engram (neuropsychology)", 2016. Briefly, an engram is a hypothetical means by which memory traces are stored. That is, it attempts to explain the permanent changes in the brain accounting for the existence of memory ("Engram (neuropsychology)", 2016, and Liu, Ramirez, Pang, Puryear, Govindarajan, Deisseroth, & Tonegawa, 2012).

Chapter 5: Transition, Trigger and the Click

A word of warning here. You may get really good on the ball machine, but there will be a transition phase from your ball machine practice to your match play. Unfortunately, you will find that when you get into match play, you may revert to your old previously-established memory paths: Old memory paths do not "go away". They are always there. What must be done is to establish a new "preferred" path that is utilized when you play. It may take several matches to make that switch (when playing a real match) to the new pathway.

It may help to try to identify a single "trigger" (some call it a cue) to help fire the new pathway. A trigger can be defined as something that tells your brain to go into the automatic mode that utilizes the new motor pathway. A trigger is the preceding event, thought, or motor action that guides your brain to use the new motor memory pathway. Even though the new path is unconscious, it can be triggered by a conscious command. When match play triggers the old muscle memory path that you do not want, you may need a new trigger to switch to your new muscle memory path that you established when using a ball machine. So perhaps a single point of focus will help. Keep talking to yourself and reminding yourself of the triggers, or cues, that initiate the whole process. Be specific and have it immediately precede the remainder of the new sequence (that is, the new motor pathway), whether it be the Get Set or the Head Turn, or whatever.

I am not the only one who thinks this helps regarding the use of triggers or cues. Coach Mike Oransky, a pro who is Director of Tennis for the city of Gainesville, Florida, for over 35 years, says this:

> *"Learn to have certain cues to help you with your strokes...*
> *In matches, when the pressure is on, everybody gets tight and less fluid.*
> *By talking to yourself, you can increase your chances*
> *to stay loose and fluid"*
> Mike Oransky

The Click

Now for "The Click". What is The Click? I would call it the moment where everything suddenly seems to go right. It becomes almost effortless. Everything, all at once – Works!

It is the Eureka moment – the Ah-Hah! You are beyond the impasse. Your efforts to establish the muscle memory – the protein synthesis, myelin formation, synaptic connections, etc. have occurred. The different chunks are finally, and seemingly all at once, operating in a smooth well-coordinated sequence. The chunks have been developed and "learned" at different speeds, but now the process really does work together. Your stroke seems automatic and effortless. The new associations have "hooked up".

Note that initially, The Click may only last 10 to 15 strokes, but as you keep repeatedly practicing that stroke you are effectively burning the processes into your muscle memory through your Muscle Memory Practice. Therefore, the frequency and duration of "the click" occurs more frequently. Realistically, you will never be perfect at all times, but you have just entered a realm where it is happening on a much more consistent basis. Something is happening that you never experienced before. Enjoy!

The best scientific study I could find that relates to this, and proves the point, is about juggling. I know (of course) that juggling is not tennis, and since this book is about "Better Tennis", why say anything about juggling? Well, the act of successful juggling is tough, really tough! The act of hitting a good tennis stroke is tough, really tough! Both are truly complex motor skills that are not easily acquired. Therefore, I reviewed a paper named "A Computational View of the Skill of Juggling", by author Howard Austin. The report describes research done at the Artificial Intelligence Laboratory of the Massachusetts Institute of Technology. In his paper, Austin notes "The single most surprising discovery made during the experiment was that for most individuals, progress was not at all continuous, but rather appeared to consist of a series of breakthroughs. These breakthroughs were not initially stable, frequently being attainable for only one or two trials, but became more frequent and stable over time. The really astonishing piece of information is that the magnitude of the breakthrough was usually 2 to 4 times that of the previous level! Jumps from 3 tosses to 10 to 11 tosses were common… Almost every subject in the experiment exhibited a breakthrough which virtually doubled the previous best effort" (Austin, 1974, p. 35).

Chapter 6: Application of Training to Your Tennis Game

Law 5: Learning different patterns back to back may cause forgetting of the initial one.

In other words, a newly practiced skill is easily broken down or diminished. It is unstable. Therefore, when you add practicing another skilled motor activity immediately after learning the first, it creates "interference". This disrupts the improvement that previously occurred. This biological fact is strong. In one study, the authors concluded that when the learning of a motor task was followed immediately by the learning of a second different motor task skill, the "subjects were unable to benefit from their previous training" (Brashers-Krug, Shadmehr, & Bizzi, 1998, p. 254). That's right, the previous training did no good. This means any and all benefit from the previous training effort were wasted.

Now let's look more closely at the academic literature:

- "The first six hours after a motor skill…is learned are crucial to formation of permanent, automatic memory for performing that skill. During these hours, the brain forms an internal model or blueprint for the skill and moves it from one part of the brain to another for storage". (University of Maryland, Baltimore, Science Daily, 1997, abstract).

- "For a short period following the initial training session, the skill is labile to interference by other skills…Interference denotes the observation that training of a new task leads to forgetting of a previously learned task" (Luft & Buitrago, 2005, pp. 205 and 209). (Note that labile is defined by Merriam Webster as "unstable or readily. . .undergoing a biological change or breakdown".)

- "The first six hours after a motor skill…is learned comprise a window of vulnerability during which the skill can be impaired or even lost by attempting to learn a second motor task" (University of Maryland, Baltimore, Science Daily, 1997, para. 2).

- "Interference with motor learning occurs when multiple tasks are practiced in sequence or with short interim periods…Analysis of movement after-effects suggested learning of the second task within 6 hours of learning of the first task led to an unlearning of the first task, or overwriting of the learning effects for the first task" (Chapman, Vicenzino, Blanch, & Hodges, 2007, p. 504, 513).

Now for a truly excellent series of experiments that gives convincing evidence supporting the fact that learning different patterns "back to back" may cause forgetting of the initial one. This study is titled, "Dissociable stages of human memory consolidation and reconsolidation", by Matthew P. Walker, Tiffany Brakefield, J. Allan Hobson & Robert Stickgold as published in Nature, Volume 425, October 2003. I consider this a "Landmark" article. The findings should change the way tennis is taught, as well as many other sports. I sincerely want to thank the publishers of Nature for their permission to go into details related to their experiment and its results. I also want to thank the authors, for accomplishing such a terrific study. I hope many of you are able to review the article itself (although it is very academic). While I do go into quite a bit of detail, the article is very well written and describes other results that are important. The figures/charts/graphs are all really well done! I hope my book helps give them all the credit that they deserve for such a fine study. I am optimistic that the reviews and citations related to this publication increase.

These experiments further confirm that learning different patterns back to back can cause forgetting of the initial one. Even more concerning is that the benefit of practice on day 1 can be lost if you practice (even briefly) that skill the next day and then follow it with practicing a different motor skill. The following experimental results detail this. The study involved 8 different groups, but to avoid confusion, I shall detail the results on only 4 different key groups:

- In the first group, it was noted that when they learned a motor task (a sequence of motor movements), then are retested on day two, there is an increase in speed and accuracy (after the overnight sleep) of that motor task, even though no further practice had occurred since day 1.
- In a second group, they learned a motor task, then learned a second motor task immediately after the first. The group was then retested on day 2. When retested on day 2, improvement occurred only for the second task (there was no improvement for the first task). Walker et al noted, "when subjects in that group were trained on a second motor sequence immediately after the first, interference was seen, so that overnight improvement in speed and accuracy only occurred for the second sequence, and not the first". The article also noted that learning the second task immediately after the first did not reverse the initial learning when retested immediately after the second task. Although the short-term memory was retained initially, it was subsequently lost.
- The third group learned a motor task on day 1. As expected, on day 2, there was overnight improvement in speed and accuracy. Further, on day 3, with no further practice on day 1 or day 2, there was further increase in speed (with a minor non-significant increase in accuracy). Simply put, if you learn a motor task on day 1, and do not practice that task (or any other task that day or the next), then you will test better for that motor task on day 2, and even on day 3 (although not as great of an improvement as on day 2). To clarify, the improvement on day 3 is additional to the improvement that occurred on day 2.
- They then tested a fourth group. This group learned the task on day 1. On day 2, they rehearsed the initially learned task and then was taught a second motor task. Results showed that learning for the first motor task had been reversed, with performance accuracy decreasing when tested the following day by more than 50%. The speed also showed a small reduction.

This is a bit complicated, but very important, so let me summarize and restate:

- You learn a motor task on day 1. Improvement in performance on that learned motor skill task occurs on day 2 (and even on day 3) even though that motor task was not practiced on either day.
- When two motor tasks are learned one after the other on day 1, then retested on day 2, there is improvement in speed and accuracy only on the second motor task (the one that was done most recently), but no improvement on the first. Improvement on the second learned motor task (the one that was learned at the end of the training session) then continues for another 1

to 2 days, even though no practice occurs. However, no improvement occurs on the motor task that was learned initially.

- Finally, a motor task is learned on day 1. On day 2, if the motor skill is even briefly rehearsed, then another task occurs, the improvement on the first task is reversed by as much as 50% (when tested the following day).

Mmmm . . still a bit unclear. Let me translate from the language of "Academic" to the language of "Tennis". The above experiment implies:

- You practice your forehand on day 1. The next day, there is improvement (when scientifically measured) beyond the practice that occurred on day 1.

- You practice your forehand (first motor task) for 30 minutes, then practice on your backhand (second motor task) for 30 minutes (both at the same practice on day 1). You have just wasted the entire practice on your forehand, at least in terms of long term retention!

- You practice only your forehand on day 1. On day 2 you hit a few forehands, then work on your backhand. The above experiment implies that because you briefly hit a few forehands on day 2, any persistent improvement in your forehand (speed and accuracy) was reduced by 50% from your previous day's practice (in terms of long term retention)

Concluding remarks toward the end note that their findings on memory lability (that is being unstable and easily subject to change or breakdown) and reconsolidation in humans complement similar findings in animal and clinical studies (they then list 6 sources).

As noted directly above, similar results related to the fact that learning of a first task being disrupted after a second task is learned on the same day, has been confirmed across multiple studies by different authors, but I will only quote a few:

- "Consolidation of motor skills was disrupted when a second motor task is learned immediately after the first" (Brashers-Krug, Shadmehr, & Bizzi, 1996, p. 252). Or to rephrase a conclusion from the same study – When the learning of a motor task was followed immediately by the learning of a second different motor task skill, the subjects were unable to benefit from their previous training (when tested the following day).

- In another article by Shadmehr and Brashers-Krug (1997, p. 409), they state, "learning of the second task leads to an unlearning of the internal model for the first".

Next is a really interesting study that further confirms the fact that practicing different types of activity after working to improve an initial activity causes significant loss of what was accomplished on the initial practice. This study was by Chapman, Vicenzino, Blanch, & Hodges (2000) involving elite cyclists, triathletes, and novice cyclists.

- They used EMG (sticking little needles into muscles to record electrical activity in milliseconds, etc.) in five different leg calf muscles to determine patterns of muscle recruitment. Note that triathletes practice 2 to 3 disciplines in one training session, compared to cyclists only focusing on one. The study showed the elite cyclists had excellent muscle recruitment, and more optimal coactivation. They had very efficient pedal strokes. Their muscle memory had learned how to perform this motor task very efficiently. However, the triathletes had much less efficient muscle patterns. In fact, their muscle activation patterns were similar to that of untrained individuals. This is despite similar training histories with comparable times spent training in cycling.

Do you realize the significance of these studies, especially the last one?! Triathletes train hard and frequently on cycling, but because they practice different disciplines on the same day, they essentially negate much of the benefit of that effort. The study refers to "muscle recruitment", which is effectively the same as muscle memory. So this means muscle memory for optimal pedal strokes did not develop because they practiced another motor skill after their cycling practice.

Therefore, AGAIN, this shows that interference with motor learning occurs when a different type of practice follows. This study also shows that the interference is not limited to a single training session, but can also have significantly negative effects related to prolonged durations of training. In fact, this study suggests that even months of training was wiped out because they had practiced different motor skill tasks back-to-back. Essentially, there was no benefit related to attempts on improving that skill (note this refers to refinement and improvement of a motor skill – Muscle Memory – not endurance training).

Bottom line: These studies are highly suggestive that if you practice multiple different strokes (forehands then backhands) back-to-back during a practice, then you are disrupting, at least in part, what you just accomplished. In fact, you may have just completely negated any benefit from the forehand practice session.

Notes

- Chinese table tennis coaches insist their students master one stroke before learning another (Greg Letts, 2007). As a group, the Chinese have a history of being the best table tennis players in the world.

- I have to admit that somewhere in life I had heard that you should not work on two things at the same time. I thought I should review this for my book. Then, when I first came across the printed, scientifically studied, statement to this (See Law #5) – I pretty much dismissed it. I thought – "Naw, I doubt that really makes much of a difference, as otherwise everybody would know about it. It can't really be much of an effect". However, my review of the academic literature shows (I should say "proves") that my initial feeling was wrong, very wrong! Multiple studies indicate this a major determinant, maybe better termed a "major detriment", in learning new motor tasks. If you practice one motor skill (forehand), then have any subsequent play or practice of another motor skill (backhand), you may have just wasted your time spent on your forehand practice. I conclude that you should apply this "Law", just like you should apply the other "Laws", to your practice session. Science says this is a more effective way. This is part of the path to "Better Tennis". This is Muscle Memory Practice.

- File under "This is even more important than I ever thought possible". Caithness, Osu, Bays, Chase, Klassen, Kawato, Wolpert, & Flanagan (2004, p. 8862) noted "full interference still occurred...when training sessions were separated by 24 hours or even one week". That's right, the study said one week. Otherwise, any play or practice (other than the stroke you are working on) will (at least somewhat) negate any benefit that you gained from your previous practice sessions! To be the purist, you should not practice anything but your chosen stroke for a full week. This means you should not play any matches, or have any hitting sessions, for the week(s) you are focusing on your chosen stroke.

- To summarize and overly simplify – To maximize the long-term improvement of a particular stroke or aspect of your tennis practice, there should be no subsequent practice of any motor skill until several days later, perhaps even a week.

Law 6: Once your muscle memory is in place it "forgets" slowly, if at all.

This is why someone who played tennis in high school or college still plays well the first time out in 20 years, even if they have not picked up a racket during that time. Muscle memory is permanent. That path does not go away. Therefore, what you have to do is make the new path, and have it be the preferred path. You do this by repeated use. The frequent use turns the new path into the preferred path. This is especially important in matches. You will initially have a tendency to return to the old memory path instead of the new one, until you train yourself to utilize the new path.

Here is some of the academic evidence supporting Law 6:

- "The memory of the consolidated skill lasts for at least 5 months after training" (Shadmehr, & Brashers-Krug, 1997, p. 409). I should note this is the minimum duration of persistence of the new learned motor behavior – they did not test after this. I could not find anything that noted performance loss occurring at a later point in time.
- Karni and Sagi, 1998, reported "Improvements in performance continued to develop over the course of 5–10 daily practice sessions, spaced 1 to 3 days apart, before nearing asymptotic performance. The skill then was retained for months and years" (as cited in Karni, Meyer, Jezzard, Adams, Turner, & Ungerleider, 1995, p. 862).
- "These changes persisted for several months". Note, this is the minimal. They do not know how long the changes persisted. (Karni, Meyer, Jezzard, Adams, Turner, & Ungerleider, 1995, p. 155).
- "Finally, there was almost no forgetting" (Karni & Sagi, 1993, p. 250).

Notes

- So how long does it take to establish your muscle memory so that it is in place, and so that it "forgets" slowly, if at all? Most everything I read indicates a 3-week period of at least every other day of practice is required. However, you can achieve definite benefit by training for a shorter period of time (say 3 times per week for 2 weeks, or perhaps 5 times in one week) of Muscle Memory Practice. But to permanently improve the odds to elevate your game, it takes concentrated practice on one shot in a concentrated period of time for probably around 3 weeks. (Again – Try really hard for every at least other day). But consider this – 3 weeks of Muscle Memory Practice to improve your cross-court forehand for the rest of your life – is it worth the time? Decide yourself if this is worth the concentrated effort.

Law 7: The temporary improvement that occurs during practice or matches should not be considered learning, but rather a transient performance effect.

As noted previously, creating muscle memory is a very dynamic process. After a single (or even just a few) session or match, any base for the improvement starts going away quickly, beginning in the 24 to 48 hour period after your practice – meaning, little if any basis for subsequent muscle memory is lost. When you practice just once, there is little muscle memory to build on 3 to 4 days later. Brain chemistry is constantly building and deconstructing all the time. Short-term memory (acquisition) erodes quickly. Per Vaswani & Shadmehr, 2013, p. 7707), muscle memory "that was acquired during training decays immediately and automatically". It only becomes long-term memory (muscle memory) by frequent repetition in a concentrated period of time.

Temporary performance improvement is an excellent thing to do 2-3 days before a match, but if you really want to really take your game to a permanent higher level, you need to have the Muscle Memory Practice. Temporary performance improvement is a transient effect – a brief reinforcement on the current pathways. It is acquisition, not consolidation. It does not establish new improved pathways. Instead it reinforces your usual game, or your previous practice session, so do not expect much more.

Notes

- Law 7 is a paraphrase of a quote from Wikipedia – Motor Learning, 2017, para. 1. The actual quote goes like this: "The temporary processes that affect behavior during practice or experience should not be considered learning, but rather transient performance effects".

- It is a bit of a leap to generalize the previously cited experimental studies and conclusions to your tennis strokes and practice. Nevertheless, the science supporting my "Laws", and their application to tennis, is pretty darn good! However, it is still all theory. Any theory needs research to determine if the hypothesis is correct. I look forward to future research studies related to all of this. I know also that the Law #5 is disconcerting. However, the current evidence is strong related to Law #5 - "Learning different patterns back to back may cause forgetting of the initial one". Decide for yourself, but I think it is certainly something to think about.

Chapter 7: How Not to Improve

Take a friend or a pro. Go out – hit some forehands, then backhands, etc. It does not matter that you did not hit that well. It does not matter if you never found a groove. After all, you got some "good" practice. You hit some balls, and got some practice in on all your shots, therefore you will get better. After all, "Practice Makes Perfect!" (At least that seems to be the thinking).

Hopefully by now, with your knowledge of how muscle memory really works, you know how wrong that thinking is. What really happened is that you practiced (reinforced) your poor to mediocre shots. Even if you did hit some better than average shots (you probably did) – was it a high percentage? Usually not. Guess what –you play the way you practice.

Or …

You went to your usual tennis practice and do the same lesson or workout. You have probably done this. After months of lessons on your entire game (forehand, backhand, volley, and serves), ask yourself, "Am I really getting better? Are your friends talking about how much you have improved? Are your opponents complaining about your shots (or their game)?"

If the answer is not a resounding "Yes", then it is time for something different. Muscle Memory Practice is critical to long-term success. This is why Muscle Memory Practice on one skill set is important for long-term improvement. Performing Muscle Memory Practice on one stroke can help you avoid practicing things that no longer deliver any benefit.

Practice does not make perfect if what you practice is "not being very good", or not improving, or many different things all at once. This is not really opinion, it is mostly science. Practice does not make perfect if what you practice on a percentage basis is being mediocre (or worse). You so have to get over the mindset that to hit a bunch of balls makes your shots better, and/or makes you a better player. Do it for fun, but do not expect to get better by doing this.

Practice does make perfect (or at least improves your skills) only if you mostly hit "better than your usual shots". Therefore, first you must learn and perfect (or at least perform it significantly better that your usual shot – or pattern). Practice does make perfect, but only if what you practice is perfect (or again – at least significantly better than what you usually hit).

I will describe another way to not improve. This happened to me recently. I was trying to redo my forehand. I particularly liked a YouTube video by Rick Macci called "Improved Forehand Technique with Rick Macci". I was trying to add more wrist-snap – some call it the wrist flip or "the flip" as dubbed by Rick Macci. (This is where you use your wrist to add a whip-like motion to the stroke). I was also trying to place the racket face down, as recommended by Rick Macci (he calls it "tap the dog"). I lost both accuracy and consistency. This was not because the information was bad (actually, the information is world class, based on an incredible amount of excellent research and analysis). The problem was how I tried to learn and apply the information. The problem was I was trying to add too many things at one time.

So I simplified. I then went back and tried to add only one new modification – "the flip". Practice started going much better! The new and simplified focus was improving my forehand. There was now minimal loss of accuracy or consistency. It goes back to trying to keep things simple. Most people can only learn one new movement at a time, especially given limited practice time. So be patient. If you are changing your stroke, work and focus on a key element that leads to the most improvement on the stroke that you have chosen to work on. Master that, then add more later.

Note: Rick Macci is a USPTA Master Professional. He has been training top athletes on how to hit. To give you an idea of what a Master coach he is, and the respect he has earned in the tennis world, let me give you a quote: "When people ask me who the #1 Jr. Coach in the world is, without hesitation I say it is Rick Macci" – Andy Roddick, n.d., page 1.

One more example of "How Not to Improve". I learned this one through trial and error. I used to push myself to near exhaustion, even having 2-hour workouts at times. I figured the more balls I hit, the better I would get. Not true!!! Due to habituation and fatigue, I was actually engraining my muscle memory with bad patterns. To make it worse, I would not practice again till the following week. Same routine. I usually would end up hitting a bit better, but only for a few days. Overall, I really was not getting much better – even after I did this for weeks! I said "Self, how is it that I am only getting marginally better despite all this effort?!?!" The answer was that pushing yourself to exhaustion on single training sessions does not do it, and once a week practice does not do it! Instead, I should have been doing Muscle Memory Practice.

Question to ask every practice…

If you practice to improve, after every practice, ask yourself this:

*Did I merely reinforce my existing muscle memory
for my usual mediocre shot?*

Or

Did I practice further to improve my muscle memory for this shot?

Muscle memory practice means that you have an extended duration of hitting the shot really well, for example, over 50% of the practice session.

Chapter 8: Caveats

1. IMPORTANT: Good health is critically important to your enjoyment of tennis. It is also fundamental to "Better Tennis". Therefore, before you begin to attempt physical activity related to tennis, especially as advocated in this book, you must be examined. You must have your planned activity approved by your physician, your pro, your trainer, and anyone else who is expert related to your health and well-being. Get their advice for how fast you, as an individual, should proceed, providing they give you approval. Also, follow up closely with that person as you work out. Do this for all sessions, but especially the early sessions. You will be hitting one shot repeatedly – probably more than you ever have in your life. It is critically important to avoid injury, especially to avoid overuse injury. This can be very hard to come back from. Gradually work your way up to the prolonged session (as long as your physician, pro, etc., approve). Do not play if hurting – seek their advice throughout.

2. Permanent is not really permanent, but the longer something is worked on then the longer the memory duration would be expected – probably months, and hopefully years depending on the intensity and duration of the Muscle Memory Practice sessions extending for several weeks.

3. Muscle memory applies to more than tennis – think learning to play an instrument, other "skill" sports, such as basketball, football, baseball, golf, soccer, etc.

4. Take lessons from a pro – learn to do it right before you change your training program. It is really hard to "reprogram", and unlearn the permanent changes. In fact, it never really goes away. Focus intensely, work diligently on the basics of good stroke production – get set, watch the ball, good footwork, follow through etc. You do not want to reinforce bad habits with intensive muscle memory practice. By taking lessons from a pro, you will ensure you are doing it right and getting the most out of your efforts.

5. Use a ball machine and take a 30 minute lesson once per week from a pro on that one shot, and then hit against a ball machine for 45 to 90 minutes practicing that stroke, 3 to 4 times per week – all for 3 weeks. (I sincerely believe that the repetition with hitting against a good ball machine is KEY!).

6. There is no Caveat #6.

7. There is no magic proven threshold for the duration of time needed to accomplish some degree of improvement. Yes, theoretically, 3 weeks is optimal to establish permanent connections, but you can achieve some benefit by training a shorter period of time (say 3 times per week for 2 weeks). Nevertheless, remember that to improve the odds to elevate your game, it takes focused dedicated practice on one shot in a concentrated (again, try really hard for at least every other day) extended period of time (several days and hopefully 1-3 weeks). But consider this – one month of dedicated practice to improve one of your shots for the rest of your life – is it worth the time? Decide yourself is this is worth the concentrated effort for one month.

8. I used a lot from Wikipedia in my research (along with other sources). Yes, I know the good and bad of this, but mostly I find Wikipedia very, very good. My book is not a true

academic peer-reviewed publication. I therefore made ready use of Wikipedia. To me, a fact is a fact. If it is a fact (true and accurate information), then I do not really care much where it came from. This is especially relevant when citing what are relatively established and accepted facts. Wikipedia is well referenced and reviewed related to accuracy. Its information and references are checked. There is a conscious effort to keep the information accurate and up-to-date. If any information is found to be inaccurate, a correction is made. I also really like what Wikipedia stands for, their vision statement: "Imagine a world in which every single human being can freely share in the sum of all knowledge. That's our commitment". Disclosure: I donate to Wikipedia every year.

9. My Laws of Muscle Memory and its application to tennis, that is Muscle Memory Practice, is only theory with no solid proof (yet?) that it works beyond my own experience.

10. I don't know what the hell I'm talking about.

Chapter 9: The Shadow Swing and the Tai Chi Stroke

"Technique is the cornerstone of this game"
Florian Meier

The Perfect Stroke

As noted, focus on one stroke at a time. The most effective way to do this is to first figure out the "best stroke" – the "perfect stroke". Figuring out the best stroke, the really perfect stroke, almost always requires lessons from a pro so that you are not reinforcing existing bad habits, or learning new ways to do it wrong.

It is impossible to know how much you should change your technique. That is up to your pro and your personal motivation (as well as how much time you have, etc.). Although it clearly would be optimal, most of us do not have the time to tackle the complexity of changing your grip, total stroke mechanics, etc. If you do, then go for it!

So discuss your goals with your pro, as well as the realistic time constraints of your life. Most of us are not going to be professional tennis players, but we do want to improve. If so, then just find a pro who can take what you have, then improve what you do in the time that you have.

But no matter what, you can still make changes in your technique that will definitely improve your strokes and overall game. You still need to strive for perfecting your stroke. No matter what you have, it can be improved upon.

The pro can give you detailed instruction on what you need. But there is also general advice that most pros do not emphasize enough (in my opinion). There is a method to improve the technique on any stroke. What is that?

You use "Shadow Swings". I believe this helps tremendously. It is so important that I consider this as a part of Muscle Memory Practice.

Shadow Swings

Practice doesn't make perfect but perfect practice really helps
Anonymous

Most all of us have heard of "Shadow strokes" or "Shadow swings". Roughly speaking, a shadow swing is moving your racket as if you are hitting a tennis ball without the ball actually being there. It is simply hitting a forehand, backhand, volley, etc., with an imaginary tennis ball. The shadow swing will train your muscles and brain to use your desired swing (or movement) for your chosen stroke. It lays down the biological path to start creating muscle memory. It sets the program and molds the mind for exactly what you are trying to establish as the preferred pathway for your soon-to-be improved stroke. A clear advantage is that you do not need to be on the tennis court. You can do this at home. Start with 3 to 5 minutes per day on practicing your shadow swing. This is a small investment of time for a meaningful return leading to Better Tennis.

More on the importance of technique and the benefit of practicing "Shadow swings":

Note that even the best players in the World are continuing to work on and improve their technique even after achieving World Number 1 status. If they do this, then the rest of us should probably spend more time making sure we get it right! Every player could achieve great technique much earlier if they would spend more time shadowing off court and less time playing on court earlier in their careers.

Novak Djokovic and Roger Federer are two recent and excellent examples of this. It is quite easy to observe the technical changes in Novak's game, especially on forehand and serve, over the past 5 or 6 years. Away from the racket area, his movement, flexibility, and defensive skills have all noticeably improved as well. Roger Federer has definitely improved his backhand recently, and appears to have returned to applying more pace to his first serve. While he was always a very good volleyer, this area also improved.

Note also the comparisons between Tennis and Dancing. Dancers rehearse or practice their skills while watching themselves in a mirror. Errors are easy to see and can be corrected immediately. The missing link for most tennis players is that in dynamic practice situations (rallying or playing points), they cannot see their technique as they practice their strokes. They are too busy trying to watch and hit the ball. What is going on here is not "perfect practice" or anything close to it, but rather the forming of incorrect and undesirable muscle memory. The longer this takes place, the more difficult it will be to change later on.

Enter "The Shadow Swing". Many pros and coaches are very big believers in the benefits of correct physical practice where the athlete will take the body through the various movements necessary to generate the best possible result on each tennis stroke, also known as shadowing. One of the best ways for an athlete to accomplish this, particularly in the beginning or early learning stages of development, is to shadow these movements or "swings", if possible, in front of a mirror. This allows the athlete to observe the entire body and, therefore, will lead to more efficient and accurate production of strokes. This has obvious comparisons to a dancer practicing their technique in the same manner. Why do dancers spend 7 or more hours per day perfecting their technique in front of a mirror? Because they are judged, to a very precise degree of accuracy, on their physical movements.

What about tennis players? Are we judged directly on our technique? No. But we are most definitely judged indirectly on our technique – by the quality of our various strokes and the results they produce.

So how long should tennis students shadow or practice their swings in front of a mirror? Coach Curtis says, "Dancers practice 7 hours per day in that manner".

Note that most of the above, starting at "the best players in the world", and ending at "Dancers practice 7 hours per day in that manner", is from Coach Casey Curtis, who is at the Curtis Tennis Academy (although I did paraphrase a bit). The material is from an excellent and interesting article written a few years ago by Coach Curtis entitled, "Federer & Baryshnikov, Perfection is No Accident". For the full article, go to this the link:

http://www.curtistennis.com/federer--baryshnikov-perfection-is-no-accident.html

Go to Coach Curtis's web site. It is on my "Highly Recommended" list. I have not been to his academy but the Web site is impressive, with some good information. Also, he coached Milos Raonic – so I think Coach Casey Curtis knows what he is doing – So Pay Attention!!!

Tai Chi strokes

Now let's add another level to this familiar concept. Let's call it the Tai Chi stroke. You perform your chosen tennis stroke, your shadow stroke, in slow motion. This is especially important in the beginning, but it has relevance at any time in your life where you are attempting to improve your tennis game, especially as related to working on technique. Working on technique is essential, and some evidence suggests that Tai Chi stroke practice is likely one of the best ways to improve your technique. Better technique translates to Better Tennis. If you want better technique, you should practice Tai Chi strokes no matter who you are – novice or pro.

Let's start with a novice – in the beginning. For example, let's say you are starting on day one of Muscle Memory Practice for your cross-court forehand. Think of this as your "core" forehand stroke. Before you actually hit the ball, start doing Tai Chi strokes. Start slowly.

Let me repeat: "Slow It Down"! Slowing it enables each aspect of the stroke to be performed perfectly. It creates the precision necessary to lay down your muscle memory. Then start your Muscle Memory Practice. Since you are starting with the cross-court forehand, this is the one aspect of your forehand stroke you must work on the longest and the hardest to make "perfect". This is the core stroke – in this case, for your forehand. Practice the one shot, with the same spin, speed, and direction from the ball machine, over and over and over.

"The circuit needs not to just be fired, but fired correctly..."
"The best way to build a good circuit is to fire it, attend to mistakes,
then fire it again, over and over"
Daniel Coyle (2009, p. 130 and 25)

You must do it correctly, and with enough repetition to establish the muscle memory. Only then can you depend on that stroke in a match. After that, once you get the "perfect stroke" down and burned into your muscle memory, then variations will come easily.

"It's all about fundamentals, getting that right,
and then the adaptations to different kinds of situations becomes easy"
Florian Meier

To get the fundamentals right, use the Tai Chi martial arts technique when trying to practice your strokes. Do your court practice, but also practice at home (more about this in the Imagery section later in the book). Go through the stroke in really slow motion over and over for at least 3 to 5 minutes per day in the beginning. Try to do this in the morning and before bedtime. Use it also before you begin your on-court practice.

Do it slowly, as you are performing your Tai Chi strokes. Slowing it down is how you learn and perfect your stroke. It is essential. It is the key. It must be precise – a Roger Federer type smoothness to your stroke.

Slow it down, then gradually automate it. Separate different aspects/positions of your stroke to 7 to 10 separate movements. You can facilitate this by using a metronome (or similar app from your cell phone). Time the metronome slowly – one click for each to your movements (remember chunking). Essentially, you are chunking your stroke into several separate and divisible parts. Break it into small pieces – indivisible units that you can understand, and reproduce reliably. Work on one unit, or one piece, at a time. Consider each unit as if it is a separate practice. Create precision – one movement at a time. In fact, you could say it is all about precision. Fix the errors. Work on the parts that you do not do well. Put everything you have into perfecting it. Have your pro watch your Shadow Stroke (using your slow-motion Tai Chi stroke).

Now tie it all together. Go for perfection. This is a rare instance when perfection is actually achievable. If one aspect of the swing is difficult (and why shouldn't it be since you never did it quite like this before), keep repeating it until it becomes perfect, then continue to repeat till it feels natural. Do not expect this to happen in one day, or 3 days, or 7 days. Improve by single steps, not by leaps and bounds. Your goal is not how fast you get there but how "perfect" your technique – your stroke – can become. If it feels uncomfortable and unnatural in the beginning, then that is a major plus – for you have discovered major flaws (in other words, you have no Muscle Memory for this movement).

If you learn how to do it correctly now, you will save time and prevent problems in the future. Acquire first, then consolidate.

. . . and, if you stay with it, it will begin to feel natural. Remember, this is how the brain learns! This is how consolidation occurs. This is Muscle Memory Practice! The control of the swing is becoming part of your muscle memory – Cool!

Now GRADUALLY speed it up.

As noted, start slowly and try for perfect stroke production. Then later speed it up. However, as I hope you know by now, once you figure out the best stroke, there still is no path. In order to make a path in motor memory you have to go over the "perfect stroke" thousands of times over an extended period of time – the optimal being 3 weeks. The more often you go over the route in a short period of time, and the more times you repeat that exact perfect stroke, then the more quickly and more permanently the "good" path will come into existence.

Then, as you practice on the court working out against a ball machine, you figure out the best route, the best stroke, by hitting it repeatedly 20 times in a row. But there still is no muscle memory. The path is not established. This is the acquisition stage. You have to go over the stroke, the perfect stroke, thousands of times over a 3 to 4 days/week for 3 weeks. The more often you repeat the "good stroke" in a short period of time, the more quickly and more enduring the path – the muscle memory – will be established. This is Muscle Memory Practice.

But I can sense you are still reluctant to do anything like "Tai Chi" (being a native Texas, I understand). You still need more convincing before you start practicing your Tai Chi-like practice strokes?

Note what Grant Grinnell writes on improving in his highly-rated book: Court Quick-Fix Booklet "Tennis Strategy: How to Beat Any Style Player":

> *"You have a four times greater chance of improving*
> *if you 'Tai-Chi' (shadow drill) your strokes in super slow motion.*
> *Three single acts of perfection twice a day.*
> *It takes 300-500 repetitions to develop a new stroke.*
> *Without Tai-Chi, students typically have to go through a relearning process*
> *because things are still happening too fast in practice sessions.*
> *The brain needs more time to engrave the full motor skill*
> *and a missed step can take hundreds of more repetitions.*
> *As a coach with over 50,000 hours on the court,*
> *at times I'd rather see my students do ten minutes of*
> *slow motion shadow drilling to fix a long-term flaw*
> *than an hour and a half of on-court play"*
> Grant Grinnell
> (location: 409 of 601)

But perhaps you need more to convince yourself that you really should try the Tai Chi stroke. Read on . . .

"Technique is Everything!"

Witness the Moscow Spartak Tennis Club in Moscow. This single tennis club in Moscow has helped train all these highly successful tennis stars. Note the success:

- Elena Dementieva – Winner of 16 WTA titles and 3 ITF titles; Highest singles ranking No 3; Won the Olympic gold in 2008
- Yevgeny Kafeinikov – Winner Australian Open 1999 and French Open 1996; Winner of 26 career titles; Highest singles ranking No. 4
- Anna Kournikova – Winner of 2 ITF singles titles, and 16 WTA doubles titles; Highest ranking No. 8; Highest doubles ranking No. 1
- Anastasia Myskina – Winner of French Open in 2004, 10 WTA and 3 ITF singles titles; 5 WTA and 3 ITF doubles titles; Highest singles ranking No. 2.
- Marat Safin – Winner of Australian Open 2005 and US Open 2000 and 15 singles titles; Highest singles ranking No. 1
- Dinara Safina – Finalist in Australian Open 2009, French Open 2008 & 2009) singles; Winner of 12 WTA and 4 ITF singles; Highest singles ranking No. 1
- Dmitry Tursunov – Winner of 7 singles titles and 7 doubles titles; Highest singles ranking No. 20
- Mikhail Youzhny – Winner of 10 singles titles and 9 doubles titles; Highest singles ranking No. 8

44

(Coyle, 2009 and "Spartak Tennis Club", 2017; "Elena Dementieva", 2017; "Yevgeny Kafeinikov", 2017; "Anna Kournikova", 2017; "Anastasia Myskina", 2017 "Marat Safin", 2017; "Dinara Safina", 2017; "Dmitry Tursunov", 2017: "Mikhail Youzhny", 2017)

Not bad! So what are key components that contribute to that tremendous success? How the heck do they do it?! How does this tie in to support the Tai Chi kind of practice? In reviewing tennis studies for my book, I found that Daniel Coyle studied the Spartak Tennis Club in Moscow. There he interviewed their coach, Larisa Preobrazhenskaya. They actively use Tai Chi strokes, except they call it "imitatsiya". (Coyle, 2009, p. 57). Daniel Coyle describes his visit to Spartak:

"I walked in to see a line of players
swinging their racquets in slow motion,
without the ball,
as a teacher made small, precise adjustments to their form"
Daniel Coyle, 2012, p. 8

"It's called imitatsiya –
Rallying in slow motion with an imaginary ball.
All Spartak players do it, from the five-year-olds to the pros.
Their coach . . . grasps arms and piloted small limbs slowly through the stroke…"
Their coach "frequently stopped them in their tracks
and had them go through the motion again slowly then once more.
And again.
And perhaps one more time"
Daniel Coyle, 2009, p. 57

"Super-slow practice works like a magnifying glass:
It lets us sense our errors more clearly, and thus fix them"
Daniel Coyle, 2012, p. 52

There must be something to this. It must be an important way to learn to hit the ball – meaning more control, more accuracy, less effort, and more speed. Some studies have shown that proper technique adds more speed to the ball than weight training and getting stronger. So strive to perfect the fundamentals of each stroke. Proper technique during Muscle Memory Practice creates strokes that are smoother, more efficient, and more effective. Proper technique reduces injury. Proper technique is Better Tennis. It is key to your success. The better your technique, the better your tennis!

In summary, you do not start with great technique; it is a life-long effort. Obviously, I have strongly emphasized proper technique, and how slowing it down is fundamental to learning technique – the Tai Chi stroke. Even the top players in the world in almost every sport still work on improving and perfecting their technique. Proper technique is key.

"Technique is everything"
Larisa Preobrazhenskaya, Daniel Coyle, 2009, p. 57

Notes

- I did think of using the term "Tai Chi tennis stroke" myself. However, in researching this book, it looks like Grant Grinnell had used it already in his 2015 book "Tennis Strategy: How to Beat Any Style Player" – so give him the credit. (Note this book is one of my "Highly Recommended" Suggestions).

- Go through the stroke in really slow motion, the Tai Chi swing, over and over at least 5 minutes per day in the beginning. Try to do this in the morning and after you get home. There is no excuse to not have time to do this at some point in the day at work. If you cannot do 5 minutes, then at least give it a go for 2 to 3 minutes before bedtime, and before your actual practice.

- "Ben Hogan, considered to have perhaps the most technically sound golf swing in the history of the game, routinely practiced so slowly that when he finally contacted the ball, it moved about an inch. As the saying goes "It's not how fast you can do it. It's how slowly you can do it correctly." (Coyle, 2012, p. 52). (Coyle, 2009).

- Again – take a lesson (and then get follow-up) from a pro. You really need to take a lesson before you start working to establish your muscle memory. Also, get follow-up and feedback from your pro as you work on developing your stroke through Muscle Memory Practice.

- I believe that any lesson or practice session, if you are really looking to improve, should be about developing "good" muscle memory – turning a good stroke pattern into something you can rely on in a match. I see so many practice and coaching sessions where, to be honest, all they are doing is reinforcing the same old muscle memory patterns, week after week. The teaching of a good stroke is absolutely critical, but unless this is translated into muscle memory, then little is gained. Fundamentals are critically important, but this is only the first step. The focus needs to be on developing muscle memory. This will require a new approach and a more effective way to teach lessons. Some smart pros will need to develop new and innovative ways to optimize how to transform the good technique into good muscle memory. I do not have the answers to this, although I think homework, effective coaching techniques, and Muscle Memory Practice would be important (for those who are really interested and willing to spend the time and energy to improve). I defer to those with far more knowledge and experience than I have or will ever have about coaching tennis. Please make it happen!

Chapter 10: Seeing It from the Outside

The Pro

Do it right before you change your training program. Get a pro. Take lessons! It is really hard to "reprogram" and unlearn the "permanent changes". Focus intensely, work on, and practice the basics of good stroke production – Get Set, watch the ball (the Head Turn), good footwork, follow through, etc.

Coaching is critically important. The pro is the outside observer. The pro sees you in a way that you cannot see yourself. You cannot give yourself the feedback you need when you are consumed on the focus and activity involved in Muscle Memory Practice (at least if you are doing it correctly). You really need their observation, experience, and insight to improve your technique and optimize your muscle memory.

> *"It's his or her ability to see you in ways you cannot see yourself – you cannot see yourself hitting the ball and will benefit from someone else's perspective"*
> Colvin (2008, p. 67)

Let your pro know what you are planning on doing. Be clear about your objectives and goals. Be clear about the process you are implementing. I doubt he/she has ever gone about teaching tennis this way, that is with Muscle Memory Practice, so be sure to review your plan. You both need to be on the same page. At the most basic level, get the lesson for the one stroke (the forehand) to one place that you are focused on (crosscourt). Take the lesson before your start, then at least weekly while you are working on your Muscle Memory Practice.

But remember the lesson does not have to be an hour. In fact, two 30-minute lessons (an initial one, then a follow-up lesson one week later would be better). Hearing a pro tell you how to do it right does absolutely nothing for your muscle memory. The pro tells you how to "do it right", but that does not make you better. Only Muscle Memory Practice does. Only repeating practice in a concentrated period of time will improve your muscle memory, Muscle Memory Practice. The focus should go from telling you how to do all aspects of the game – to a focus on actually developing muscle memory by a focus on only one stroke (the forehand) and one component of that stroke (the cross-court).

Then supplement your pro's lesson by using a ball machine. Have the pro watch you as you hit against a ball machine. This obviously better simulates your practice and should help your learning curve. You need their feedback for Better Tennis.

One other really important "To Do" item: Start keeping a Tennis Log (or you can call it a Tennis Notebook, if you prefer) of what you learned, and what you will be primarily focused on in your next workout. Start your Tennis Log today! (I mentioned this earlier but it really is important.)

The Coach

I have hopes that maybe some tennis pro/coach (at least one) will read this book. Therefore, I am passing along a few, very few, coaching tips. It is simply advice on how one of the greatest coaches of all time taught. I consider this a Best Practice model. It is information as noted in an incredibly important article that should be mandatory reading for every coach and/or pro. The article is "What a Coach Can Teach a Teacher, 1975-2004: Reflections and Reanalysis of John Wooden's Teaching Practices by Ronald Gallimore and Roland Tharp as published in The Sport Psychologist, 2004, 18, 119-137".

I can summarize my advice in in three easy steps:
- Read the article.
- Reread the article AND take notes.
- Turn your notes into action – make it happen!

Some additional information from the article:
- John Wooden would devise practice drills specific for each player's needs.
- His teaching utterances/comments were short (4 to 5 words), punctuated, and numerous. He rarely spoke longer than 20 seconds.
- Demonstrations were rarely longer than 3 seconds.
- Instructional statements were brief. Be concise and quick. Do not string things out.
- Most of what he said we categorized as "Instructions". Of 2500 hundred things recorded, most were just plain information about how to play basketball. 75% was information about the proper way to do something.
- Much was repetitive. He wanted things to become automatic – reached through repetition and increased speed.

I kept the above to less than 100 words. The article itself is almost 20 pages long. There is so much rich material for any coach in this article. If you are a coach or a pro, if you care about effective teaching on any level, then please read this masterful "How to" work. Take notes, then turn those notes into daily actions. You will be better because of it!

Notes
- Many feel instructions work best when coaches only use 4- to 5-word instructions – keep it concise, objective, clearly stated and easily remembered. (See Highly Recommended chapter for the article on John Wooden.)
- A pro will see it the best. There really is something for a trained expert to analyze your game. Of course, the key is to find the right person and to explain what you are trying to achieve

and how you want to go about it. The pro needs to understand how much you can realistically change your game, given your mindset and time limitations. If you choose not to utilize a pro, then at least video record yourself while at practice. Then watch the video on the courts or study it later when you get home. In fact, it might even be helpful to video record your teaching session with your pro.

Chapter 11: Homework

We need to change the way we learn to improve our tennis game. To do this, it is important to practice after a lesson. Put another way, there must be homework!

Think of it as taking a college course. You hear the professor talk (for tennis this would be a lesson from a pro) in a lecture. Yes, you learned something, but not much. Real learning comes from doing the homework, from doing the practice!

Take the lesson from the pro, but then work on laying down muscle memory by doing exactly what the pro tells you. Learn to do it right, but then do it at least a thousand times after you are doing it right (and before you next lesson). It is the Muscle Memory Practice that makes perfect, not the lesson.

You should have made notes in your Tennis Log on what your pro wants you to work on. Now – Do Your Homework! When you do Muscle Memory Practice, you should add notes on how your session went and what you learned.

Notes

- Your homework is Muscle Memory Practice
- Work with your pro to devise a list of the 7 most important aspects of stroke making. (See my list of 7 principles in the next chapter). Prioritize the list – rank the most important components first. The three most important components should be the top three. Think of these as Keystone Habits. Now spend 90% of your time in dedicated practice on the first three. Learn how to do the first three as perfectly as possible. Then continue to practice only the first three over the next 3 weeks – to really establish muscle memory. Once that is laid down as muscle memory, then move on to the next three. Work on items 4 to 7 for the next three weeks etc. Spend 90% of your practice time on the most important points of stroke making. So I made my list. I think it may also work for you – read on!

Chapter 12: Fundamentals and Repetition

The GOATs

"Mastering the fundamentals is often the hardest and longest journey of all"
James Clear (2015, August 14, last sentence of article)

Let's start with the streamlined version of the definition for Fundamentals.

Fundamentals

adjectives

- being an essential part of, a foundation

noun

- a basic principle...that serves as the groundwork of a system; essential part (dictionary.com)
- determining essential structure or function; of central importance (merriam-webster.com)
- a core component or fact upon which other aspects are built. A fundamental fact is a fact that is vital, and must be known before secondary assumptions or conclusions can be drawn (businessdictionary.com).

The greats of the game have good fundamentals.

"The biggest thing we should take away from Federer's forehand –
It's all about the fundamentals"
Florian Meier

Few things are as important as a focus on the fundamentals. Mastery of the fundamentals can be the key difference in winning or losing a match. It can determine the result of the third set tiebreak. As will be noted in a future chapter, even 1% gains can be a significant difference.

Perfect the fundamentals and it will help carry the rest of your game. This is especially important in the beginning. However, even after years of experience it should be a primary focus of your practice.

A good tennis stroke is complicated. There is always something to tweak – something to work on. There is always a need to optimize – to improve. But there are essential components, and there are at least of 100 minor refinements. Sometimes we focus too much on the minor stuff. Unfortunately, these details can distract us from the only essential thing: Hit the ball well. A complicated athletic feat still comes down mostly to doing the fundamentals well.

"Complexity is the enemy of execution"
Tony Robbins, 2014, p. 41

One of the fastest ways to make progress on creating good strokes is to focus on one key component of a good stroke. So eliminate the refinements. Do just one part at a time – just one key critical fundamental part of the stroke. This does not mean just one practice session. It means a focus on this fundamental, over and over again, through multiple sequential practice sessions in a concentrated period of time. That is Muscle Memory Practice.

Burn into your muscle memory the most important part of the fundamentals.

Sometimes, after you focus on what is fundamentally important, you will note that suddenly progress comes much more quickly. This is because you are now fully committed to a goal that was only getting moderate attention previously. Consider the goal – to commit to master the most basic aspects of good tennis strokes – the Get Set, the Head Turn, and hitting the Sweet Spot.

Focus on fundamentals and repetition – it is important beyond words. But do not believe me – See what two old GOATs say and do!

Let's start with perhaps the GOAT (Greatest Of All Time) of all football coaches.

Vince Lombardi

Vincent Thomas "Vince" Lombardi was an American football player, coach, and executive in the National Football League. He is best known as the head coach of the Green Bay Packers during the 1960s. He coached his team to three straight and five total NFL Championships in seven years. He won the first two Super Bowls following the 1966 and 1967 NFL seasons. Lombardi is considered by many to be the greatest coach in football history. The NFL's Super Bowl trophy is named in his honor. He is recognized as one of the greatest coaches and leaders in the history of any sport ("Vince Lombardi", 2017, para. 1).

He assumed the players knew nothing, even after winning dominating seasons. He would start with the most basic concepts. When the Packers lost the championship game in 1960, in the book, "When Pride Still Mattered" by David Maraniss, the author notes on page 316:

"He took nothing for granted.
He began a tradition of starting from scratch,
assuming that the players were blank slates
who carried over no knowledge from the year before.
He began with the most elemental statement of all.
"Gentlemen", he said, holding a pigskin in his right hand, "this is a football"

There was repeated emphasis on the fundamentals, even starting with how to block and tackle. That season the Packers beat the New York Giants 37-0 to win the NFL Championship.

Some core beliefs by Coach Lombardi were established by his mentors. Again, as recorded in David Maraniss' book, "When Pride Still Mattered" was this statement by Colonel Earl H. "Red" Blaik of Army (page 163):

"Through the years I have found that between equal teams the winning formula is a thin margin above which to remain requires fidelity to fundamental principles"

Now let's continue with the GOAT of Basketball coaches.

John Wooden

John Wooden was an American basketball player and coach. He won ten NCAA national championships in a 12-year period as head coach at UCLA, including a record seven in a row. Within this period, his teams won an NCAA men's basketball record 88 consecutive games. Wooden was named national coach of the year six times. He also won a Helms national championship at Purdue as a player 1931–1932 for a total of 11 national titles. He was the first person to ever be inducted into the Basketball Hall of Fame both as a player and as a coach ("John Wooden", 2017, para. #1 and 2).

Now some John Wooden quotes on what he thought was important. The first one is from the book "Wooden: A Lifetime of Observation and Reflections On and Off the Court", page 140, 2010. The next two are as cited in AZQuotes:

*"I believe in the basics:
attention to, and perfection of,
tiny details that might commonly be overlooked.
They may seem trivial, perhaps even laughable
to those who don't understand, but they aren't.
They are fundamental to your progress in basketball, business, and life.
They are the difference between champions and near champions"*
John Wooden

*"There are no shortcuts.
If you're working on finding a short cut,
the easy way, you're not working hard enough on the fundamentals.
You may get away with it for a spell, but there is no substitute for the basics.
And the first basic is good, old fashioned hard work"*
John Wooden

"The importance of repetition until automaticity cannot be overstated
Repetition is the key to learning"
John Wooden

What about Wooden's coaching techniques? There was a huge emphasis on repetition. There was emphasis on drilling. The guys had the basic skills down cold. It was all muscle memory. There was no thinking involved. The basic skills were automatic. Practicing and drilling until the players' actions were automatic was critically important. Mastery of the fundamentals was paramount.

Did John Wooden think repetition was important? Note his "Laws of Learning":

"The four laws of learning are explanation, demonstration, imitation, and repetition. The goal is to create a correct habit that can be produced instinctively under great pressure. To make sure this goal was achieved, I created eight laws of learning; namely,

"Explanation
Demonstration
Imitation
Repetition
Repetition
Repetition
Repetition
and Repetition"
John Wooden, 1997, p. 244

This is the direct quote. This is not a typo! My computer did not get stuck in a loop, and my paste function did not malfunction. Wooden believed repetition was critically important. Even after you repeated it, he believed it should be repeated again and again. This is Muscle Memory Practice!

Every good tennis stroke can be boiled down to essential components. But first start with the fundamentals and doing it right. It is the fundamentals that must be mastered. Perfecting the most basic principles is what truly works. Repetition in a focused, concentrated amount of time, aka Muscle Memory Practice, is the ticket. It is the most simple components of stroke production that most of us lack, and that is what holds many of us back.

"There is a simple checklist of steps that you can follow right now
—basic fundamentals that you have known about for years—
that can immediately yield results
if you just practice them more consistently"
James Clear
(2015, March 31, under section "Use What You Already Have")

"Success is often a result of committing to the fundamentals over and over again"
James Clear
(2015, April 9, para. 9)

Chapter 13: The 7 Principles

The Most Important Things to Think About

I really believe in my 7 principles, especially the first three (Get Set, Head Turn, and Sweet Spot). They should help no matter what your grip or style of play – whether orthodox or not. They should help your focus. They should help everyone from novice to pro. It is all about the fundamentals! They should help you whether or not you get lessons from a pro (but I highly recommend a pro).

Study and Apply!

The first three are critical – really critical: Spend 90% of your effort and concentration on them for your first 3 week period (again, for ease, I suggest starting with a prototypical cross-court forehand). Do not forget to really work on the basics (see chapter on "Fundamentals"):

1. Get Set (get your racket back before the ball crosses the net, get your feet properly set) before the ball crosses the net.

2. Turn your head.

3. Find the Sweet Spot – focus on hitting the sweet spot on your racket – EVERY TIME.

4. Rotate: Use the left hand above the right hand to guide the racket back, then rotate both shoulders to the right. (This is a forehand stroke and assumes you are right-handed.)

5. Follow through.

6. Start slow and smooth.

7. Think about the middle part of the stroke and controlling the racket when doing your stroke.

"Everything should be made as simple as possible, but not simpler"
Albert Einstein
(BrainyQuote)

I believe these are the 7 most important components of good strokes. Of course, this could be argued endlessly, and should make for good switch-over discussion at your next tennis match, but at least give this a go. All I am really hoping for is perhaps helping you find something useful!

As noted, I consider the first three critical. They are more important than all else. I consider these three to be "Keystone habits". "Keystone habits start a process that, over time, transforms everything". This is described in Charles Duhigg's excellent book, "The Power of Habit". In it he tells how Paul O'Neill became CEO of the Aluminum Company of America, Alcoa. When he took over, Alcoa was having many problems. Within about a year, "Alcoa's profits hit a record high. By the time O'Neill retired in 2000, the company's net worth was five times larger than before he arrived". It also "became one of the safest companies in the world". So how did this happen? O'Neill believed that "some habits have the power to start a chain reaction, changing other habits… Some habits matter more than others… These are 'keystone habits' … Keystone habits start a process that, over time, transforms everything. Keystone habits say that success doesn't depend on getting every single thing right, but instead relies on identifying a few key priorities…The habits that matter the most are the ones that, when they start to shift, dislodge and remake other patterns" (O'Neill, 2014, Chapter 4 para, 16-22).

On #1 – "Get Set"

The Get Set is very important. It gives you the time to make a smooth fluid stroke. With good body position and early preparation, you can deal with variation due to spin, speed, and bounces. It also allows for maximal racket head speed, and more accurate powerful strokes.

So how should you go about this? First of all, you need to determine what your Get Set position is. Work with your pro. To further clarify, think of your Get Set position like a still photo. There should be no backswing or any type of backward movement from the set position. There should only be forward motion.

It is very important to realize that even if we know our Get Set position, most of us do not Get Set quickly enough. Why? I think this is because there is not a clearly-defined moment/time when the Get Set position should occur. We have all heard you should Get Set before the ball gets to you, but does it mean before or after the bounce? If before, then how much before?

Note that early preparation is key! Per Brabenec and Stojan (2006, p. 7), the "stroke preparation … can increase or decrease the timing and coordination with regard to the optimal contact point. Having a good preparation will increase the chance of making contact at the optimal contact point and achieving the desired result with regard to speed and placement of the stroke". So to clarify and provide a goal related to early preparation, I recommend to Get Set before the ball crosses the net. This gives a clear parameter to strive for. I have found that defining very specifically when this is to be done helps my game. My primary purpose here is to remove any subjectivity from it. This provides a way to self-judge and self-regulate whether or not you are doing it correctly. If one is giving lessons, it also provides an objective parameter for instruction.

On #2 "Head Turn"

"Watch the Ball". It is the number one rule of tennis. It is probably the most frequently stated instruction by coaches, parents, and even to oneself. How many times have we heard it? How many times have I chastised myself for repeatedly not doing this?

So let's face up to the truth: It is easier said than done. Most of the time we are watching the ball, just not very well. Also, when students hear it, they respond, "I am watching the ball". We all really believe what we are saying. This is because we believe we are watching the ball – and it is true – we are. However, we see it through peripheral vision. We are not looking directly at the ball, which is what our coaches are all trying to get us to do.

Now, how can we make this easier to achieve? First we need to remove any subjectivity from the "Watch the Ball" dictum. Again, as we described in the Get Set description, we need to clearly identify when we do this successfully and when we do not. So, what to do? How do you correct this? Everyone says watch the ball, but no one ever tells us how to watch the ball. Enter the Head Turn principle. With the Head Turn, the head (of the tennis player) makes a visible and noticeable turn toward the racket and ball at the point of impact. If done correctly, then the player's nose should be pointing directly to the point of impact between the ball and the racket. This is how to watch the ball. This is objective – there is no subjectivity about it. The nose points the point of impact, or it does not. That simple!

It has been said that nobody watches the ball better than Federer. I would also add that nobody does the Head Turn as consistently and clearly as Federer. Don't believe me? Then Google the "Ultimate Slow Motion Compilation" on Roger Federer (provided for free by Essential Tennis). Watch his "Head Turn". Note that sometimes he even turns his head <u>before</u> the ball strikes the racket! His head turn is a conscious move. Because of it, he watches the ball better than anyone else. I believe his Head Turn is part of what makes him the leading contender for the GOAT (Greatest Of All Time).

Now, continue to watch after Roger strikes the ball – his head remains fixed! I call this "<u>The Federer Pause</u>". With this, like Federer, you can objectively check yourself to determine if you really are watching the ball. That is, like Federer, you should be looking down at the court at the place after the ball was hit. Watch how consistently he does this. Burn it into your memory!

By doing the Head Turn and the Federer pause, you will watch the ball. There should be no more yells of "Watch the ball!" No more telling yourself to watch the ball, but never quite doing it. No more replies from students that they were watching the ball, when you know they were not. Now there is something clear and objective, a concrete physical action, to achieve one of the most fundamental aspects of Better Tennis. Now you can easily and quickly determine if you are doing it correctly. Now a coach can watch a student to see if the head turns, and if the student's nose is pointing toward the impact point of the ball and racket. It does not matter whether it is a forehand, backhand, or volley, the principle of the Head Turn should always be visible.

Finally, when we think or hear "Watch the Ball", we know how to make it happen!

On #3 The "Sweet Spot"

It is important to hit the ball in the Sweet Spot of the racket. This is physics. Note two things: First, any time the ball is hit off center, the racket angles in that direction – meaning if you hit in the bottom part of the racket, then you are more likely to hit into the net. Next (and more importantly), any time the ball is hit off center, the shot loses significant speed and power. That is, you lose control. The slower ball speed means (especially if your hit it in the lower part of the racket) that you are more likely to hit the ball into the net.

So how much power do you lose by hitting off center? How much does this really alter the shot? A LOT!!!! Want an example? Let's start with power. We all love to hit "power shots". In order to really understand this, you will need to go to the Tennis Warehouse University Site (web link is http://twu.tennis-warehouse.com/cgi-bin/comparepower.cgi). Choose your racket, then see how much power you lose when you miss the Sweet Spot. Let's say you miss the Sweet Spot by maybe 2 inches. The power falls off by about 25% on most racquets. That is HUGE! That is the difference between "netting the ball" vs the ball zooming over the top of the net for a deep shot. That is the difference between a poach by your opponent vs a successful winning shot. Note also the torque of the racket and loss of power means loss of accuracy and consistency. Also, to be consistent, you need to hit in the same part of the racket as much as possible. So if you really want to hit with power and accuracy, do not freak out on your string tension. Instead, focus, I mean REALLY REALLY focus and concentrate, on consistently hitting the Sweet Spot!

Start watching other players. Note that most of the time they hit into the net, they hit in the lower part of their racket. Any time the ball is hit off center, the racket torques and angles in that direction. This means if you hit in the bottom part of the strings you are more likely to hit into the net, especially when you consider that makes the racket unstable and the ball goes slower.

Also, the Sweet Spot (think the stability and power) of the racket moves toward the direction of the force. Now let me explain what this means. Perhaps this can be best understood by using a "thought experiment". If you drop a ball from a standing position on the court, it leaves a perfect circle. Now imagine using "Hawkeye" or "Shot Spot" to describe the mark of your racket hitting the tennis ball. Most players would imagine a perfect circle on the racket. This would be true if you hit flat shots, but most of us do not – we use spin.

Before going further, recall Hawkeye being used during a match. A point is disputed. Hawkeye is used to resolve the contested point. There is no circle on the ground. Instead there is an ovoid, or ellipse. This is because the ball strikes the court at an angle. The ball undergoes compression, deformity, and rolls. Hence the area of contact is an ellipse.

Now imagine what happens when you are hitting a topspin shot. The ball strike point with the racket is angled because the racket is going from low to high. When the ball initially strikes the sideways upwardly-moving strings, there is deformity and compression on the ball, and the strings give. The ball rolls again. If you were to put Hawkeye on the strings, the point of contact would not be a circle. Instead, the area of contact would be in the shape of an ellipse – just like when the ball hits the court during a point.

Most of us try to hit in the center of the racket, but considering the above, and if you are swinging from low to high to hit topspin, then the initial hit of a topspin shot would be wrong. Think of the true contact points (that is, "area") of when the ball is on the strings. If you are hitting with topspin, and the initial point of contact (the first part of the ellipse) is the true center of the strings, then the end of the ellipse would be below the center of the racket. In fact, all the point/area of contact with the racket would be below the midpoint or center of the strings. Therefore, the ball is more likely to lose speed and the racket turn – meaning the ball has a higher probability of going in the net (primarily due to loss of speed rather than racket torque).

To hit a balanced shot, the initial point of contact needs to be somewhat on the skyward side of the string center (if you are hitting topspin). If you can imagine the ovoid/ellipse of "Hawkeye" on the strings of the racket, then you can also visualize why your initial contact should NOT be the center of the strings, but actually slightly above the center of the racket. Because the area of contact is an ellipse, and not a circle, the initial point of contact should be slightly skyward of the racket center, so the center of the contact area (or ellipse) is equally above and below the center. The only way for this to happen is to have the initial strike point be slightly above the center fo the strings.

So really try hitting the sweet spot. This requires focus and effort. As described above, this will maximize power and accuracy. Remember, if you are just two inches off the sweet spot, then you lose 25% of your power. That's huge! Even worse, the angle of your racket face turns. Therefore, if you want a controlled, accurate shot, you need to consistently hit the Sweet Spot. As always, it will take focused practice (Muscle Memory Practice) to achieve this.

Trying to hit the Sweet Spot may even help us to watch the ball better (goodness knows that helps too) and to hit more consistent powerful shots, and therefore have Better Tennis!

On #4 – Rotate and Use Your Non-dominant Hand

I have a friend who is a technical editor. He reviewed and helped edit my book. He found the #4, as written above, a bit confusing, so here is a further expansion. Essentially, this is part of the Get Set. This involves rotation of the non-dominant hand/shoulder. Use the left hand above the right hand to guide the racket back, then rotate both shoulders to the right (this is the forehand and assumes you are right handed).

The rotation and use of the non-dominant hand steadies the rest of your stroke. This pulls both your shoulders back and winds you up like a spring waiting to uncoil. Watch the pros. In hitting their forehand, they almost always use the opposite hand to take the racket back behind the shoulders – that is, greater than 90 degrees. Further, when they run for the ball, even a drop shot, the racket is not flailing randomly. Watch how they often still keep their non-dominant hand on the racket to keep it steady. They then place the racket in the proper Get Set position for the next shot. (See sections on Get Set and Head Turn for further details.)

I also use my non-dominant hand to set the angle of my racket face – meaning if I am tending to hit the balls in the net, then I set the angle more open. Conversely, if I am hitting it long, then I close the angle. I know this sounds weird, but it helps me and provides a really useful "correction technique" if I am hitting into the net or too long.

On #5 – Follow Through

On the other principles, I state things differently, or at least have a different point of emphasis or perspective. I do not really have a lot to say about the follow through, except it is really important (just talk with any pro). It reportedly helps power, accuracy, decreases injury risk, adds consistency, helps maintain proper technique, etc. Also, many pros recommend accelerating through the ball; in other words, the maximum racket speed as you are striking the ball. This is a key part of the follow-through. Perhaps the best example is simply to watch video of your favorite pros. Compare what you do to what they do. Watch and learn.

On #6 – Start Slow and Smooth

I have a tendency to jerk my racket around when I am trying to hit hard. Of course, hitting hard is all about racket head speed, not muscling it through. The slow smooth start and swing, with consciously thinking about the middle part of the swing makes for more consistency and control. It also looks a heck of a lot better – more Federer-like.

On #7 – Middle Part of the Stroke

This may be a bit confusing, so let me clarify. I hear pros talking about getting set and following through. I agree very much. But there seems to be much less emphasis on what I would call the middle part of the stroke. I would define this as the 4 inches before and after the point of contact with the ball. Those 0.004 seconds the ball is in contact with the strings determine the result of that stroke. Of course, I know that contact point is determined by getting properly set up, stroke technique, speed, path, and angle, of the racquet head and ball, but surely there should be some focus and concentration related to the most critical moment of the entire stroke. Per Brabenec and Stojan (2006, p. 6-7), "coaches and players have been paying attention in training or during the learning process exclusively to the visible elements of the stroke: backswing, forward swing, and follow through… but the real efficiency of a stroke depends strictly on the moment of contact/contact point… [and that] almost single-handedly decides the fate of the stroke". They also note, "if the ball makes contact with strings 5 cm off center, the stroke will lose 30% of its intended speed". Concentrate on controlling the racket, especially the angle of the racket, through that narrow part of the swing. Even more importantly, totally focus on racket control the moment the strings hit the ball.

Notes

- When practicing with the ball machine, I have said to Get Set before the ball crosses the net. However, to facilitate initial learning, exaggerate this for your first few practice sessions against the ball machine. Get Set (think being a statue like the photo that your pro determined as the set position) before the ball even leaves the ball machine. Then, when you get comfortable and proficient at this, start in your neutral position. Now use the Get Set before the ball comes across the net.
- I know that the pros do not have a single stationary Get Set position. Instead, the movement is fluid – some would call the motion a swoosh. However, for the vast majority of us, I believe the concept of a relatively stationary Get Set position is useful, especially in the beginning. For the pros, I will defer to their expertise as to their idea of a Get Set position; if you're a pro, please send me your thoughts.
- In the first two principles (the Get Set and the Head Turn) I tried to remove subjectivity out of self-observing (or observing others) as much as possible – that was my goal. This gives you a clear and very objective marker to test yourself (or others) and thereby to determine if you are doing it correctly. For the Principles of the Get Set and the Head Turn, the criteria to judge if you have (or have not) done this is so objective that you do not need a pro to be sure you are doing it correctly. Get one of your tennis friends to help. Heck, the objectivity of this is so straightforward that one does not even need to play tennis to judge if done correctly or not. Remember, an important aspect of practice is immediate feedback so that you can attend quickly to your mistakes. If you do not have someone to help you, then try to videotape yourself and review between ball machine loading sessions.

- As I said, I consider the first three principles to be really critical. Re-read about Keystone Habits, Chapter 13. You should spend multiple practice sessions totally dedicated to the first three. Remember, you can only work on one thing at a time. It works best if you add only one new element to your game. Then get that consolidated into muscle memory. Then add another technical improvement. It just will not work well if you are working on your footwork, your shoulder, your follow through, the angle of your racket, etc. – all at the same time. Remember the Einstein quote at the beginning of the chapter – "Everything should be made as simple as possible, but not simpler".
- So my "7 Principles" may be only "theory", but I really do find them useful. Consider giving it a try. Also, your pro can probably take it to the next step, as to what is useful for a 3.5 player but may not be useful for a 4.5 player.
- Some further points on "Watch the Ball". Actually you should take it further. You should not focus on watching the ball. Focus on only one part of the ball. Specifically, you should focus on a single part of the ball – just the small area of 1/2 inch (1cm) contact point that is needed in order to hit/place the ball exactly where you want it to go.
- Some further points on the Sweet Spot:
  - First, the volley. Watch Federer volley in slow motion. He almost always hits off center – just a bit skyward and toward the end of the racket face. I have tried to incorporate this and it does help. Remember to do the Head Turn, even on the volley – Federer does.
  - Next, I have also watched the pros hit their ground strokes in slow motion. In contrast to what I recommend, they usually hit in the bottom (groundward) side of their racket face. Therefore, this must be better. Tennis Warehouse University has an interesting academic article related to this.(http://twu.tennis-warehouse.com/learning_center/location.php). To quote the site, "In fact, low impacts had an average of 53% more topspin than high impacts. This result was astonishing enough that the experiment was performed four separate times using slightly different setups, but with the same results each time"). Bottom line – hitting low on the racket imparts more spin. Nevertheless, I still find I do better when I hit my ground strokes a bit further skyward and beyond the center of the racket face. Perhaps it is just a stage in my development and I have not become accomplished enough to control and benefit from hitting in the groundward side of the racket. So I recommend to try both and see what helps your game. (Note when you focus on this that you are also watching he ball much better).
- I readily acknowledge these principles, especially the way I describe the Get Set (and others), may not be textbook classic, but they help me. I want to emphasize that I am sure at least some of my theories are wrong (see "Caveats"). However, some will be useful. One of my favorite sayings is "All models are wrong, some are useful" ("All models are wrong, some are useful" 2017, para. 1). To better fit this book, I have changed this saying to (Spoiler alert – I conclude the last chapter in the book with this):

All Theories Are Wrong, Some are Useful.

I sincerely hope you find something useful!

Chapter 14: The 80/20 or 90/10 Rule

There are so many minor technical things that add up to a really good tennis stroke. I sometimes believe that we spend too much time on the more minor stuff. There is much too little emphasis on the most important. It is something akin to the 80-20 rule – also called the Pareto principle or the Pareto analysis.

Pareto analysis is a formal technique useful where many possible courses of action are competing for attention. In essence, the problem-solver estimates the benefit delivered by each action, then selects a number of the most effective actions that deliver a total benefit reasonably close to the maximal possible one. Pareto analysis is also a creative way of looking at causes of problems because it helps stimulate thinking and organize thoughts ("Pareto analysis", 2017, para. 1 and 2). The Pareto principle is also known as the 80/20 rule, the law of the vital few, or the principle of factor sparsity ("Pareto principle", 2017, para. 1).

To paraphrase, simplify, and make it more relevant to this discussion – roughly 80% of the problems with you strokes comes from 20%, or just a few, things that you are doing wrong (or at least need to improve significantly). Therefore 80% of your effort to improve should focus on just a few key fundamental core concerns.

I actually would take an even more extreme view when approaching this. I would propose that 90% of your effort should focus on the most basic, fundamental and important aspects of good tennis strokes – such as the Get Set, the Head Turn, and Hitting the Sweet Spot (the Keystone Habits).

Therefore, 90% of your lesson and practice (especially in the beginning) should be spent on what reliably creates consistency and control. Your focus should be narrow: maybe only one thing, and certainly no more than 3. So what are the most important aspects of stroke production? Just as a starting place (although yours may be different from mine), let's take the top 3 of the 7 Principles – the Get Set, the Head Turn, and the Sweet Spot. I now ask you – Has anyone spent an entire lesson only on Getting Set? How about just a third of the lesson? Has anyone spent an entire lesson emphasizing and practicing just "watching the ball" (or as I think is a more effective way of putting it – the Head Turn)? How about a third of the lesson? Has anyone practiced this much time totally focused on hitting the Sweet Spot of the racket? The answer is almost certainly a resounding "No!" Therefore, when we get in match what do we do? We do not get set very well. We do not watch the ball very well. We hit off center.

How could it be otherwise? We do not have muscle memory in place to do this. We have not trained ourselves to do this. We have not practiced enough to consolidate it in our muscle memory. We have put in enough time, that is Muscle Memory Practice, so that we consistently and reliably do this.

"Your odds of success improve when you are forced to direct your
Energy and attention to fewer tasks.
If you want to master a skill – truly master it
You have to be selective with your time…
You have to focus on a few essential tasks"
James Clear
(2015, July 17, under section "The Underrated Importance of Selective Focus")

Notes

- Vilfredo Federico Damaso Pareto was born July 15, 1848. He was an Italian engineer, sociologist, economist, political scientist, and philosopher, now also known for the 80/20 rule, named after him as the Pareto principle ("Vilfredo Pareto", 2017, para. 1) (very interesting character – I recommend you read more about him).
- I know I already mentioned my three key principles as Keystone Habits but this is a really important concept, so let me repeat: The habits that matter the most are the ones that start a process that transforms everything else. Mastering a Keystone Habit starts a chain reaction that accelerates improvement on all other patterns of muscle movement (Muscle Memory) for Better Tennis. Master these and everything else improves.

Chapter 15: Transference

You may feel you are neglecting or hurting the rest of your game as you focus on only one aspect of one stroke for 3 weeks (for example, only the forehand cross-court shot) but that is usually not the case. Let's say you only hit forehands for 3 weeks. You may be surprised to find that even though you did not hit any backhands, your backhand stroke improved. In fact, there is pretty good scientific evidence that your backhand could improve, even though you only practiced your forehand. Why?

From personal experience, when I was working on my forehand cross-court shot, although I did not hit any backhands or volleys, both the backhands and volleys also definitely improved. I think this is because I was so focused on Getting Set (getting my racket back before the ball crossed the net). Also, as I practiced, I started developing muscle memory, doing a Head Turn, really watching the ball, and hitting the Sweet Spot. I also had focused on a smooth stroke and following through. In effect, the other strokes improved because I was doing the "Fundamentals" (actually The Keystone Habits), which apply to all strokes. I really had started to automatically perform the most important rules of good stroke production on a better, more consistent level. I therefore did this even on the shots I did not practice, and the shots improved.

So I researched this further. The results show there is science to back up the proposal (theory) that if you focus totally on one shot, you may not be hurting the rest of your game and may actually be improving other strokes. My experience was the result of an observed scientific principle called "Positive Transference" (Seidler, 2010; University of Minnesota Duluth, n.d.). This means when you practice and learn one skill, then improvement occurs in a related skill. The learning of one skill set is helpful in learning another skill set. Additionally, previous learning of skills, such as the Get Set and the Head Turn, acquired while practicing your cross-court forehand, transfer to when you start working on your backhand strokes.

A further component of Positive Transference is called the "Bilateral Transfer of Learning" (Teixeira, 2000). This means that tasks and skills learned in one limb are thereafter acquired more quickly in the other limb. In other words, if you have learned how to hit a better forehand, then your backhand will also improve to some extent, even though you have not practiced your backhand.

The transfer occurs because there is a strong cognitive component. The first part of learning a new motor skill is telling yourself what to do to learn this new skill. You have to think to make it happen. Therefore, when one skill set is learned, the acquisition and consolidation of the second skill set is easier. I also strongly believe that some, but not most, components of good stroke technique can be transferred from the forehand to backhand side, and vice versa.

This is especially true for those skills that are learned in the cognitive phase. This means you are consciously telling/training yourself to do it differently. The conscious thoughts of the brain are planning the actions of the upcoming motor movements. Skilled motor tasks, especially in tennis, have a anticipatory component that is separate from the motor task itself. The ball is coming toward you. You anticipate and calculate the angle, speed, spin, etc. You need to figure out the proper distance of the ball from the body in order to hit it correctly. None of this is a motor action. It is all cerebral. It is all cognitive. Academically, this is sometimes referred to as "anticipatory timing".

Transfer of learning from one arm to the other, the left to the right and the right to the left, has been observed to take place with hitting a ball with a racket (Teixeira, 2000). This is in large part due to learning to "anticipate" what is going to happen and what you will need to do when you see the spin, speed, and direction of the on-coming ball – the ball's trajectory, height, etc. Your brain calculates and anticipates. You then Get Set as part of that anticipation in getting ready for the next shot. Again, all this relates to anticipatory timing (and planning). Then the Head Turn and Sweet Spot kick in (hopefully). These are still part of the self-conscious instruction and movement due to anticipating the path and movement of the ball and your upcoming stroke.

The transfer of anticipatory timing is relatively strong, although the transfer of the actual motor movement itself is weak. The critical aspect is starting the movement at the right time. Note this is not just theory, as it has been shown that the transfer of anticipatory timing control worked for both sides of the body, with "both hands benefiting similarly from previous practice with the contralateral hand". In fact, related to this anticipatory timing, both hands "demonstrated the same capacity to maintain approximately 70% of the level of performance achieved with the contralateral practiced hand" (Teixeira, 2000).

This means, simply put, if you work on your forehand, the anticipatory skills that you learn will transfer, in part, to the backhand side, and if you improve on your backhand, then your improved anticipatory skills will transfer, in part, to your forehand.

Also, this obvious fact should be stated: The brain, although frequently divided into a right and left hemisphere, is one organ. One side of the brain freely communicates with the other. Any motor skill has a cognitive and a motor component. These skills, especially the cognitive skills, are readily transferred from one side of the brain to the other.

In essence, the brain transfers the "knowledge" (although not the specific motor movement itself) gained in obtaining the new skill set to a new situation that was not specifically practiced. That is, the skillsets you learned when hitting your forehand are now available, at least partly – and in a good way. These skillsets are already present when you begin hitting your backhand. Your positive performance in hitting your forehand is now positively influencing your backhand and volley. Neat!

So do not fret excessively that you are spending all of your practice time on only your forehand for 3 weeks. You may be surprised that your other strokes will not suffer, and could actually improve!

Chapter 16: Troubleshooting
or Back to the Basics

As discussed previously, I try not to exert myself too much in the hot Texas summer. So last summer, for about three weeks, I was hitting backhands and volleys. I usually would do this with two rounds of each. I would go out to maybe 2 times per week (yes I know, this is not Muscle Memory Practice – but I was working really hard, it was hot, and I did not have the time).

At the end of three weeks, I felt I was not improving. So I went back and reread what I had written. I then realized how wrong my practice was. I may know my theory, but I was not practicing it. So I changed. I started hitting 4 to 5 rounds of <u>one</u> shot only. I started with volleys. Within the three sessions, there was clear improvement. However, I thought something still was not right. It did not seem to be "clicking" as well as it had in the past.

I reviewed my theory again. I realized my practice habit was significantly wrong. The mistake I was making was that for volleys, I had set the ball frequency to a higher speed (as it does not take as much time for volleys). I figured if I hit more balls per hour, then I would get more practice per hour, and therefore improve more. Again – I realized how wrong I was!

Remember, it is not just about getting a lot of reps. It is about doing it right. A lot of reps does establish muscle memory. But I was learning to do it wrong. I was establishing the wrong, that is the bad, kind of muscle memory.

Remember, you first need to create, to learn and <u>acquire,</u> the perfect stroke. You need time to think about your stroke. You need to work on your fundamentals, your technique. You need to be sure you're getting set up properly, time your Head Turn, focus on hitting the Sweet Spot, bending the knees, keeping the wrist below and in front of the racket head, etc.

You need time to review your stroke, to check yourself, to see if you are indeed doing it correctly. If you hit a bad shot, you need time to analyze and fix what you just did wrong. If you are lucky enough to have a pro or friend, they need time to tell you what you need to focus on to correct the next shot. Work not just on repetition, but repetition focused on hitting the perfect shot. Then when you <u>acquire</u> that skill (you know muscle memory by now) repeat 1000 to 3000 times – to <u>consolidate</u> it.

So I slowed it down, and worked on form (you know – the "Tai Chi" way of doing strokes). There was enough time between ball machine feeds that a I could practice a "Tai Chi" stroke. I thought about, and focused on hitting correctly. Shortly after that, there was another "Click" (not earthshaking, but definitely present, and a clear step forward).

Once you can perform your stroke consistently at a slow speed, then speed it up a little. If your shot breaks down, then slow it down until you correct that weakness. <u>Consolidate</u> and strengthen your Muscle Memory Practice on fixing the weakness, on removing the imperfection. Once you fix it, then hit it 1000 times; then you can speed up again.

Live and learn – "Back to the Basics".

Notes

- Remember to work only on one thing at a time. See chapter on "How Not to Improve".
- It is far better to hit 100 shots where you are totally focused on improving your technique on every shot, than to hit 200 balls where you are just slapping it around or 400 balls on 4 different shots.

Chapter 17: More on Practice and the Importance of Repetition

One of the most constant and consistent points of emphasis in the book is the importance of practice and repetition. This is certainly true for "Better Tennis", but it is also true for many other things. Rather than go through a narrative, I have provided some quotes below from famous successful people:

"It is through this sheer number of repetitions
that you'll come to understand the fundamentals of your task...
you can begin to simplify.
because you know what is essential"
James Clear
(2015, August 14)

"Perfection will come through practice. It cannot come by merely reading instructions..."
"Both success and failure are largely the results of habit!..."
"Greater skill is developed through practice and experience...."
"With persistence will come success"
Napoleon Hill (2012, pp. 48, 84, 119, and 156)

"Repetition is the mother of skill—that's where mastery comes from—"
Tony Robbins (2014, p. xxv)

"The ultimate mastery is physical mastery.
That means you don't have to think about what you do; your actions are second nature.
And the only way to get it is through consistent repetition"
Tony Robbins (2014, p. 42)

"It's Not the Work, It's the Re-Work...
The best athletes actively critique each repetition and constantly improve their technique.
It is the revision that matters most"
James Clear
(2016, March 7, under section "It's Not the Work, It's the Re-Work")

It can take 3000 or more repetitions to commit the simplest of movements to muscle memory,
and up to 20,000 to make a complex skill movement "permanent"
Terry Laughlin (2009, January 14, para. 1)

Notes

- Terry Laughlin coached three college and two USA Swimming club teams from 1973 to 1988, improving each team dramatically. In that time, he developed 24 national champions at all strokes and distances – the first national champions produced by four different teams! His swimmers also earned world rankings (Laughlin, 2008).
- Have you seen the video of Odell Beckham Jr (a premier NFL receiver) making one handed catches? Some would argue he has made some of the greatest catches of all times. You know how he does it? HE PRACTICES the one-handed catch!

Chapter 18: Mike Leach and Repetition

I really like Coach Mike Leach. He may not (yet) be a GOAT (I hope I do not offend you, Mike by not calling you a GOAT), but he is certainly successful. He is currently the coach at the now successful Washington State football program. He is tremendously successful wherever he goes. From 2000-2009, he coached the Texas Tech football team offenses to lead the nation in passing six times and total yards three times (Brunt 2017). His teams were not filled with the recruits that line up at Alabama or Ohio State. His successes were the result of his coaching schemes, based on his practice sessions. He is unique. He is intelligent. He "Gets It"!

So what does he think about repetitions?

What are some of the key elements to his coaching philosophy?

> *"The rarest commodity you have is reps"*
> *"Do it over and over so he really learns"*
> Mike Leach
> (2012, October, para. 5)

How about some more observations?

> *"He spent an entire practice period perfecting one play"*
> David Purdum
> (2012, October, para. 4)

> *"They must get enough repetition to get the execution in muscle memory*
> *so that they don't have to think during the game.*
> *The execution becomes 'instinct'.*
> *In order to get enough repetition*
> *you must not have too many different things for the players to learn*
> *and you must structure practice to maximize repetitions...*
> *Every part of practice were designed*
> *to give repetitions to the important techniques"*
> Jonathan (2014, para. 21, number 8)

> *"Leach and his coaches spend most of their time relentlessly drilling"*
> S. C. Gwynne (2009, around para. 35)

> *"Everything is about repetition"*
> Cody Hodges (2009), Leach's 2005 starting quarterback
> (as cited by Gwynne, 2009, around para. 30)

Chapter 19: The Ball Machine

I noted in the "Caveat" section to use a ball machine. Why?

The ball machine can provide the endless repetitions that you need to perfect your strokes via Muscle Memory Practice. Today's ball machines can provide just about any shot, spin, and speed that you want to work on. It is that simple.

Also, I love hitting against the ball machine. It is a great workout, much preferred over going to the gym or running 2 to 3 miles (at least to me). It is also somewhat of a Zen experience. At work and home, there is always something going on – always someone to talk with and interact with. On the court with the ball machine, it is peaceful. It is quiet. There is nothing to break your focus or concentration – just you and your hitting against the ball machine. It is a wonderful break in the day. Since you are by yourself, and probably no one is really watching, you can experiment and try things you never would otherwise. It is a great thing to do. It is an additional path of discovery.

Remember that part of deliberate practice is reaching out – trying things that are on edge of your ability. Work with the ball machine to try different shots that you need to improve, then choose the one that you believe will help you the most if you master it. It can be related to consistency, placement, power, angle, etc. You choose what you think will most help your game. You need to determine the basic technique of strokes that you need to work on. Again, it needs to be something that pushes the edge of what you can do. The ball machine enables you to do that. No embarrassment if you fail miserably or look foolish. After all, you are by yourself. No one is watching. You also discover little tricks and tips that help your game. It is a learning experience.

Also, this will noticeably improve your game. Another advantage is that you will not have to ask your pro to feed you 600-700 balls to your forehand for 60 to 90 minutes. That would test the limits of even the most patient pro, and it would really be expensive.

So why aren't you using the Ball machine???

Hopefully by now you are convinced. However, it is important to remember, when you hit against the ball machine it is not just about the repetitions, it is really about problem solving. When you make an error, then determine the cause of the error and fix it. It is the focused problem-solving practice (always trying to improve on the stroke) that makes it time well spent. For example, when working on the cross-court forehand, focus also on always hitting the ball deep, with spin, angled, and of course some different amounts of power and touch too. You are not just trying to get the ball in for 20 times in a row. What you want to do is to hit a really good deep shot with accuracy and pace (in this particular case, as other times you may be working on a sharp angle with touch) 20 times in a row. That kind of shot and consistency can win matches!

Use a ball machine and take a 30 minute lesson once per week from a pro on that one shot, and then hit against a ball machine for 45 to 90 minutes practicing that stroke, 3 to 4 times per week (4 times is best) – all for 3 weeks. (I sincerely believe that the repetition with hitting against a good ball machine is KEY!). Count how many times in a row you can hit that shot without missing. The goal is to hit it 20 times in a row (OK – I just made that up), or at least multiple times without missing, per round. So count your shots. This also puts extra pressure on you. Unfortunately, you will find you might tighten up when you get to the 15th or 16th in a row. This helps simulate match conditions and provides you some extra practice in working through pressure situations (although of course this is much less than in a real match).

In the beginning, learn the core stroke first (for example, a cross-court forehand). Start with an "average" forehand stroke – meaning medium paced, medium spin, medium height. This will be your core stroke. Learn the core stroke really well. You are trying to perfect your technique on this stroke as much as you can. Your fundamentals should be so solid! With this forehand stroke, you should have amazing consistency (a nice, fairly deep, reasonably paced stroke with some spin). Get this one down! After you learn this, variations will come more easily. Proper technique with attention to the fundamentals for that core stroke will forever make variations and adaptations come much more easily. As Florian Meier says, when discussing "How to Hit Your Forehand like Roger Federer",

"It's all about fundamentals, getting that right,
and then the adaptations to different kinds of situations becomes easy"
Florian Meier

Remember you are working on Muscle Memory Practice. **Try really hard for at least every other day over the next 3 week period** – **all on one component of one stroke – such as the forehand cross-court (not forehand down the line).**

As you improve, then practice moving around! Practice that one shot but also practice moving – side to side, rushing the net – but all cross-court forehand. Practice shots coming at you fast and low, slow and high, topspin and underspin, etc. Give it variety, but keep it all on the one shot (for example the cross-court forehand), but importantly focus on variants of the cross-court forehand for several sessions. Once you get that variation down (that is, hitting it 20 times in a row multiple times per ball machine session), then try another variation.

I should remind you that Andre Agassi trained using the ball machine (although if you read the book, you know that it was because his father forced him). He was especially grilled on hitting the ball early, hard, and on the rise. Andre's stories and consistency are legendary. This skill set was a key factor in his success. Sessions against the ball machine probably helped.

If you love tennis and want to get better, then the ball machine is a great tool.

"High repetition is the most important difference between the deliberate practice of a task and performing the task for real when it counts"
Geoff Colvin (2008, p. 69)

"The most effective deliberate practice activities are those that can be repeated at high volumes"
Geoff Colvin (2008, p. 70)

Ball Machine Drills

Stand, Walk, Run

How do babies learn to run: They start by standing, then they walk, then they learn to run. Start with the simpler task and then incrementally build on it. That is, each task should progressively become harder and involve a higher skill level. You lay each foundation layer on top of the preceding foundation. Make sure the foundation is good before you move up to the more difficult level. **Make Sure** you master hitting the ball standing still before you start to move a few steps at a time – then master that level – then make the distance run greater – perhaps side to side or front and back (but only one). You should master that level (20+ strokes without missing on a somewhat regular basis) before going to the next level.

Patterns

Depending on your skill and level of play, you will need to design different drills for yourself. If you are a 3.0-4.0, then probably start by the ball machine hitting to you while you stand at the same spot. As you are able to hit 20+ in a row on a regular basis, then program the machine to where you have to move around, all the while hitting your forehand (or whatever you are working on).

Obviously, you can design drills to where you practice a sharply angled cross-court, or a power shot, to the corner of the deuce court. Remember, you do not move on until you can do that shot consistently – that would be 20+ in a row, several times, per round/load of balls in the ball machine.

If you are really good, and are consistent in moving around and hitting 20+ shots that are sharply angled (or power rocket-like balls to deep in the court, or whatever you are working on), then step it up! If you are a 4.0-4.5 or better, and already have consistency, then challenge yourself.

Practice patterns – ones that are similar to real-life match scenarios. You really need to challenge yourself by adding more difficult drills. Perhaps challenge yourself with patterns – ones that better simulate match play. Start with patterns of two. For example, program the ball machine to feed both of the deep corners of your court – deep to your backhand and deep to your forehand. You then practice hitting the shot back down the line. You practice this pattern. You do Muscle Memory Practice by hitting nothing but forehand down-the-line, then backhand down-the-line, then forehand down-the-line, then backhand down-the-line, etc. Then repeat thousands of times. If you practice this for 3 weeks, then returning a really fine shot down the line should become second nature.

I do not care what level of play you are currently at – even the top 10 in the world. You can design a drill that will tax the edge of your skills and abilities. There is a pattern you and your coach can design that will help you win matches if you master it. The ball machine can be programmed to give you this pattern over and over and over and over; and then you begin to nail the pattern. Punish yourself and push your limits. Make it where you have to hit the ball on an all-out run, then speed back to the other corner of the court, then back again. If you get really good at that pattern, then think what that will do for your game, your match play. It can greatly increase the odds of your success.

Or . . . if that does not ring your bell, then consider this: Maybe you can win more matches, but only if you take shots with higher risk – say a sharply angled cross-court. Unfortunately, right now, when you try this, there may be too many unforced errors, but you CAN fix this!

Do this pattern, or practice this shot, for 45-90 minutes per day for 3 weeks. Do Muscle Memory Practice! Again, you will get good! With Muscle Memory Practice, you can get really good at this, your so-called, "risky shot". But if you can hit that shot really well and consistently, then that shot is no longer a risky shot – because now it is part of your arsenal! It is a relatively safe shot because of the consistency with which you can now perform it. It is now in your muscle memory – that is, "performed without conscious effort" (the very definition of "Muscle Memory"!). In reality, you are creating a game where the odds are in your favor!

> *Don't practice until you get it right,*
> *Practice until you can't get it wrong*
> Anonymous

Remember, a critical element of Muscle Memory Practice is that you keep repeating that shot after you get really good at it. This will take self-discipline/self-control. It may even be boring. But consider, do you want to take your game to a permanent higher level? To do so you must build muscle memory. So you are to the part where you are now hitting well – REALLY WELL. But this is where the importance of Muscle Memory Practice time kicks in. Now you must consolidate this so it becomes permanent. To accomplish this you must hit an additional 3000-5000 balls, or more. Remember the quote from Joiner and Smith (2008, p. 2949), "after reaching a high level of performance…additional training that has little effect on performance can lead to substantial improvements in long term retention".

Simply put, the more the repetition of hitting well, the more likely permanent changes develop that will keep you hitting well, especially when you need it. You are training yourself to play better during a match because most of your time and practice was spent training your body to constantly and successfully hit the (so called) "risky shot", or the pattern that previously gave you problems.

Do you think this will help your match play? Sure! But I bet you do not realize what a significant difference it could possibly make.

Read the next chapter to learn more!

Notes

- It ain't risky if you can hit it repeatedly and consistently under adverse conditions.
- Remember the chapter on "Application on Training to Your Tennis Game – Laws 5-7"
- Recall – to really do Muscle Memory Practice, it takes concentrated practice on one shot in a concentrated period of time – for at least 3 weeks. But consider this – one month to improve that one particular "risky shot" – or that one selected pattern with precision and consistency, for the rest of your life – is it worth the time? Decide yourself if this is worth Muscle Memory Practice for one month – to improve your game FOREVER!

- How about the service return?
  - Beginner and intermediate players should set the ball machine so that it delivers the ball to different areas of the service box (and place the machine settings where there are different speeds and amounts of spin). Then practice your service return.
  - Even if you are a pro, this can help. They now have towers that will hold a ball machine. The ball machine can deliver 120 mile per hour serves to any location in the service box, with right or left spin, and/or topspin or underspin. Do this an hour a day for three weeks and I would guess your service return win percentage would go up significantly. If you are a pro and almost always hold your serve, then why in the world would you not strictly follow Muscle Memory Practice to improve your service return (remember the importance of Law #5)?!?
- You should work 70% of the time on your strength (Bollettieri, 2001, page 364). He knows more than I do – no doubt about it! But everyone is different. If you lose because your weakness is really awful, then obviously you need to strengthen that. If do not win because you cannot finish points, then that is what you need to work on. What to do? How to decide? Simply keep track of the numbers of winners and unforced errors you have in a match (or a set – whatever you can track). If you are a pro, then that is easy, as they keep match statistics. If you are a typical club player, you probably know without giving it much thought. Go crazy and have a friend keep stats, then do the same for your friend. Then get analytical. Identify where your mistakes are occurring. Are you hitting short or long? Too high or too low? Is it due to poorly hit cross-court backhands or down-the-line backhands? Not coming to net enough? Volleys (or lack thereof)? Then really practice trying to fix the mistake. (Note – casually hitting a bunch of shots does not really improve your game). If your number of winners is considerably lacking compared to other players of similar caliber, then you need to develop an offensive weapon (via Muscle Memory Practice – of course). Develop more power, or precision, or angle, etc. If you have more unforced errors than players of similar caliber, then you need to start with that. Remember, your practice needs focus. Develop, then master your new skill. Then after you have acquired this skill, continue to hit that same shot for an extended period of time, several days (at least another 3-7 sessions – more is better) so that the motor action becomes consolidated, that is, it becomes muscle memory. Make your past mistakes the foundation of your future success.
- I know hitting against a ball machine is not the same as hitting against a player in a match. Nevertheless, it will really help. A rough rule of thumb I use is that if I can hit a particular shot 20 times in a row against a ball machine then I expect to hit that same shot consistently 10-12 times in a row in a match. (I have no studies or stats to back this up – just an educated guess).
- A very quick informal review of ball machine rental rates revealed one rate in Austin of over $30 for one person to rent for 90 minutes (Ouch!). Can't afford to go back there again. (Of course, if it were half that price, I would probably go back multiple times). Kind of pricey I think (but maybe not to many others). Additionally, to me, this is a strong deterrent to taking lessons from a pro, in that I cannot afford to do my homework on the pro's recommendations, so why bother? However, other places were more reasonable. A check at the Gainesville Tennis Academy in Florida gives individual rates of $47.40/month, $132.50/quarter, and $212.00/year. So of course, local rental fees will vary. I would hope some of the more pricey rentals could be modified. Maybe they could offer an option for

unlimited sessions (limit of 60 to 90 minute per session) for use of the ball machine for a 1 to 3 month period (or perhaps a bundle of 10 to 15 sessions for a much reduced rate). The price could even be tiered to allow a cheaper rate for non-busy times. All this would greatly benefit the local tennis community and increase the ball machine use (as well as making more money for the tennis center). Courts or country clubs could offer a package deal of several brief lessons by the local pro (on your chosen stroke/one aspect of stroke). Then you "do your homework" by practicing against the ball machine, doing what your pro suggested; then return in a few days (or one week) for another pro lesson; back to the ball machine for homework; then back to the pro, etc. Since the ball machine rate would be substantially less if packaged with a grouping of pro lessons, this would likely be appealing to many of us tennis players. The student would likely see more benefit and improvement. Heck, the pro would probably like it too (imagine a student coming back just one week later, having practiced your recommendations by hitting 1000-1500 balls!). All this would hopefully be done in conjunction with using the principles of Muscle Memory Practice (including working on one stroke). It seems like an obvious win-win to me (but this is just another "theory").

- Some say that hitting against a ball machine is boring. If so, I doubt you are making the practice session a real challenge. Challenges are not boring. So step it up. Challenge yourself. (Of course, some will still find it boring. If that is you, then keep doing what you already do, and see Chapter 26).

- What to do if you do not have availability of a ball machine, or it is beyond your budget? You may be highly motivated to do Muscle Memory Practice against a ball machine, but simply cannot afford it. Unfortunately, there is no easy answer. You can always hit with a partner. You can both hit the same cross court, or perhaps one cross court and the other down the line. You could also practice volleys, but herein lies a problem. I see most people practice their volleys by hitting back and forth to each other. In other words, the person in the backcourt hits to the net person, then the net person returns the shot to the backcourt person. The obvious problem is that you are training your muscle memory to hit it back to your opponent instead of putting the ball away (or practicing your passing shots). Now your muscle memory will do this automatically in a match because this is how you practice. Even with a crosscourt practice (with both people in the backcourt), you are practicing hitting to the other person, instead of trying to elevate your game and hit better shots that your opponent cannot manage . . . but I digress. Back to the original question. I do not have a satisfactory answer. So sorry. I can only hope the tennis centers and clubs can better serve the tennis community by offering more affordable rates. It also seems like frequent rental at lower rates would be more profitable than a few rentals at high rates, but I do not really know how the numbers add up…I can only hope! (Note, obviously I am strongly advocating for change, as suggested in the paragraph immediately above and this one. Again, we can only hope!)!

Chapter 20: The Sven Simulator:
A Little Goes a Long Ways

Have you ever noticed how close the numbers of winners are in a pro match? Maybe you watched TV, perhaps a "Slam" match on TV. At the end of the match, they sometimes give the number of points won – the match statistics. Did you ever notice how often it is incredibly close in terms of number of points won/lost? The higher ranked player usually wins the match, but in reality, the winning player does so by winning maybe 2 to 4 points more shots out of 100 points, when tallied over the entire match. This is often the case. Why is that? How can it be so close, yet the better player almost always wins? How can they win so often by literally less than handful of points?

First a little background on statistical probability. We tend to think that if you flip a coin, you get two heads in a row, and then the next flip will probably be tails. But it is much more complicated than that. To best explain this, I am going to defer to Sven. He is one of my best tennis friends. He graduated with a degree in Mathematics from Humboldt University of Berlin (Yes – a German mathematician). After that, he did years of computer programming and working with software. He now heads a team at Amazon.

Sven knows statistics and probability. He knows computers. He knows how to calculate statistical probability outcomes. He tells how his statistics professor told the story about other students. The professor had half the class of students make a chart predicting the sequences of heads or tails, regarding 100 coin flips. The other half of the class recorded the data on 100 actual coin flips. The professor could nearly always tell, at a glance, which chart was based on predictions, and which was based on real outcomes. The real outcomes chart had significantly longer sequences of heads and tails than the charts the students predicted.

Now remember, this is a simple coin flip. It is a 50-50 chance. But the same is true for tennis players of equal ability. So a meaningful question would be – What are the results, in terms of games won and match scores given two players of very similar ability – say when one player wins 51% of the points? The answer is that you can end up with is longer runs of winning and losing than you would anticipate.

This seems like an easy-to-understand statement, but in order to really appreciate and understand the significance, you will need the Sven Simulator.

To use this tool, you will need to go to his Website – http://www.jayoogee.com/mytennismatches/Login.aspx. He used his Website primarily to keep track of his scores (you can too – see notes at the end of this chapter), to analyze his games, and to establish trends and patterns. Being a math and computer guy, he played around.

He wrote a "Simulator".

You enter whether it is a 3 or 5 set match (or more accurately, does it take 2 sets to win or 3 sets to win the match). You next enter the percentage of points won out of 100 points played. For example, one player wins 51% of the points.

The Simulator then does a variety of calculations for 100 games using statistical probability.

Results show total matches and games won and lost out of 100. Results also calculate the score for each individual match – all based on the statistical probability of one player winning 51% of 100 points. Results vary – a lot! – Much more than you would think.

It is all fact. It is all statistical probability and outcomes. It varies far more than you would expect. Let's look at it all more closely. Start by running a simulation of Player 1 winning 51% of the points and Player 2 winning 49% of the points. Behold the results:

Simulation Results

Matches Won Player 1:   59

Matches Won Player 2:   41

No.	Score	No.	Score	No.	Score	No.	Score
1	7-5, 4-6, 6-2	26	5-7, 6-4, 3-6	51	6-4, 3-6, 6-3	76	4-6, 4-6
2	5-7, 7-6, 7-6	27	4-6, 4-6	52	6-4, 2-6, 5-7	77	7-5, 6-3
3	6-3, 6-3	28	1-6, 6-2, 6-2	53	7-5, 6-3	78	6-3, 4-6, 6-3
4	7-6, 3-6, 7-5	29	3-6, 3-6	54	6-7, 3-6	79	3-6, 6-3, 4-6
5	4-6, 6-4, 4-6	30	7-5, 4-6, 4-6	55	6-3, 7-6	80	6-2, 6-7, 6-7
6	6-4, 6-3	31	3-6, 4-6	56	6-0, 6-3	81	6-3, 3-6, 4-6
7	7-6, 6-2	32	5-7, 6-2, 5-7	57	7-5, 7-6	82	6-4, 6-2
8	6-2, 6-3	33	1-6, 4-6	58	6-4, 6-7, 7-6	83	3-6, 4-6
9	0-6, 6-3, 6-7	34	6-4, 6-3	59	1-6, 6-1, 6-0	84	6-2, 6-1
10	6-2, 7-6	35	6-4, 6-2	60	4-6, 6-0, 3-6	85	4-6, 6-3, 6-3
11	1-6, 0-6	36	6-3, 5-7, 6-2	61	7-6, 6-3	86	6-7, 1-6
12	2-6, 6-3, 7-6	37	6-4, 3-6, 6-3	62	6-3, 7-6	87	4-6, 4-6
13	3-6, 6-2, 7-6	38	6-4, 6-0	63	3-6, 6-1, 7-6	88	6-4, 4-6, 2-6
14	1-6, 7-5, 3-6	39	5-7, 1-6	64	7-6, 7-6	89	6-4, 6-3
15	3-6, 4-6	40	6-7, 2-6	65	6-2, 6-2	90	6-3, 6-2
16	6-7, 5-7	41	6-3, 3-6, 6-3	66	6-0, 3-6, 7-5	91	6-4, 6-2
17	6-3, 6-4	42	4-6, 6-2, 6-1	67	4-6, 6-2, 4-6	92	6-4, 6-3
18	7-6, 6-4	43	5-7, 1-6	68	4-6, 2-6	93	4-6, 6-3, 6-3
19	4-6, 7-5, 6-1	44	6-3, 4-6, 2-6	69	7-5, 6-7, 6-1	94	5-7, 6-7
20	4-6, 6-4, 6-7	45	6-2, 7-5	70	4-6, 1-6	95	7-5, 6-7, 7-5
21	6-4, 6-2	46	6-2, 7-5	71	6-4, 6-7, 5-7	96	2-6, 3-6
22	2-6, 3-6	47	4-6, 6-2, 7-5	72	6-3, 7-5	97	6-3, 4-6, 7-6
23	6-2, 6-7, 1-6	48	4-6, 3-6	73	3-6, 6-3, 7-6	98	6-7, 1-6
24	7-6, 5-7, 6-0	49	4-6, 6-4, 6-4	74	1-6, 2-6	99	6-1, 7-5
25	6-3, 7-5	50	6-4, 6-4	75	4-6, 6-3, 6-4	100	5-7, 6-7

To repeat, Player 1 wins 51% of the points and Player 2 wins 49% of the points. Player 1 only wins two more points out of 100 than player 2. Out of 100 simulated matches, Player 1 wins 59 times out of 100 matches.

Now let's run some more simulations. On a 51% winning percentage, running 5 groups of 100 matches, your number of matches won shows the following results: 59-41, 66-34, 63-37, 51-49, and 60-40 – with the low 51-49, the high being 66-34, and the average being 61% winning.

Now do the same calculation for 50%, 51%, 52%, 53%, 54%, and 55% (using Player 1). The numbers are as follows for 6 simulations:

- 50% is 55, 52, 44, 47, 49 – for matches won, with a low of 44, the high being 55, and the average being 49.8% winning
- 51% is 59, 66, 63, 51, and 60 for matches won – with the low 51-49, the high being 66-34, and the average being 61% winning
- 52% is 68, 76, 77, 68, and 81 – for matches won, the low is 68-32, the high is 81-19, and the average is 74% winning
- 53% is 78, 85, 78, 77, and 76 – for matches won, the low is 76-24, the high is 85-15, and the average is 78.8% winning
- 54% is 87, 89, 81, 87, and 86 – for matches won, the low is 81-19, the high is 89-11, and the average is 86% winning
- 55% is 91, 90, 94, 84, 95 – with a low of 84, a high of 94, and an average of 90.8%

See the domination by the player who wins 54% of the points – a difference of only 8 points out of 100. It seems so hard to believe that a difference of only 8 points out of 100 will result in match domination (roughly almost 9 out of 10 matches), but that is how it is according to statistical probability.

Back to the title of this chapter, "Sven Simulator: A Little Goes a Long Way". To illustrate what this means (again based purely on mathematical outcomes predicted by statistical probability), use the simulator again (or just look at the above). The percent of winning matches for winning 50% of the points is, of course, about 50%. Now note the same for the player winning 53% of the points 78.8% – Impressive!

So I propose that by simply improving your game, through Muscle Memory Practice, on 1 to 2 particular shots, that you should be able to add at least 3 winning points out of 100 to your match statistics, and improving your winning percentage from 50% to almost 80% against players of similar skill.

Truly "A Little Goes a Long Ways"!

Notes

- Sven commented to me that his simulator is able to perform more complex simulations than the "simple" one above. You can also enter the service advantage, and he recommends doing some simulations that take serve advantage into consideration. The way you do this is, for example, setting the player 1 to 59%, and player 2 to 55%. This way both players have 5% advantage when they serve and a 4% difference. It is also explained in the blue information icons on the web site.

Sven also recommends investigating how the simulations differ between best of 5 sets and best of 3 sets.

- I need to point out that I doubt any of your friends will notice you are now winning 54% of the points instead of 51% of the points. What actually happens is that you have fewer unforced errors. What also happens is that your shots go a little faster, with slightly more angle, and a bit deeper in the court. You get more "forced errors" from your opponents. They blame themselves, rather than really notice that their errors are due to your improved shots, your Better Tennis! However, when you get to the 10% better, then you start getting the extra attention and compliments on your improvement.

- I would like to emphasize how important Sven's simulator is, and the useful analytical tool it can become. Consider the advantage of calculating current statistical odds for any tennis player – from Bob or Betty at the public court, to a top 10 player at a slam. See what the odds are of winning when Raonic or Isner serves versus the opponent. Note that the serve advantage can change depending on the effectiveness of that serve against that particular opponent. Learn to understand how the odds change with a small improvement (or worsening) of the serve; even though the small statistical change may not be apparent to observers, the outcome of games and matches will be real.

Chapter 21: 1% Better

The Concept of Marginal Gains

Need more convincing that small differences can add up to big results? Read on…

David Brailsford was the Performance Director of British Cycling. Prior to his tenure, no British cyclist had ever won the Tour De France. Then Brailsford took charge and applied the concept of "Marginal Gains". The results: His team won the Tour De France four times. He also orchestrated England winning 18 gold medals in the Olympics ("Dave Brailsford", 2017). Brailsford is credited with championing a philosophy of "marginal gains" at British Cycling:

> *"The whole principle came from the idea that if you*
> *broke down everything you could think of that goes into riding a bike,*
> *and then improved it by 1%,*
> *you will get a significant increase when you put them all together"*
> Dave Brailsford
> (As quoted by Matt Slater, 2012, para. 3)

The concept of marginal gains has also been applied to other sports with success. So how to apply Brailsford's approach to tennis?

Small (really small – as in 1%), seemingly insignificant improvements have a way of adding up and creating major improvements with dramatic success. Almost every aspect of your tennis stroke, the bad and the good, is the result of how you practice and play. So eliminate the bad by replacing it with the good. Let's face it, you will not make enduring 5 to 10% improvements in 1 to 2 days. You are really unlikely to achieve a 2% improvement in 2 to 3 days. Therefore, be patient. Apply the concept of marginal gains. Strive for 1% improvements. Over time, this creates success! It works!!!

To summarize, small wins in technique and consistency, especially established through Muscle Memory Practice, build up over time to improve your game and winning. They build on each other. Not a viscous cycle, but a virtuous cycle with improvement and success adding to each layer, and ultimately "Better Tennis".

Notes

- The concept of marginal success is also referred to by some as "small wins". In Charles Duhigg's excellent book, "The Power of Habit", he notes, "A huge body of research has shown that small wins have enormous power, an influence disproportionate to the accomplishments of the victories themselves" (Duhigg, 2012, chapter 4, section 2, para. 12).
- Other authors write about the concept of marginal gains. I particularly like the writings of James Clear – see my "Highly Recommended").

Chapter 22: It Isn't All Mental

I propose that many of the claims of mental errors –
lack of confidence, lapses in attention, lack of focus, etc. –
are the results of muscle memory,
or more accurately, the lack thereof.

Now – I can almost hear the verbal barrage: "How can you not say it is not mental?!" So, before I drown in a deluge of protest, let me point out that I agree that some unforced errors are mental. Sometimes it is clearly and obviously a "mental" error – say you double fault on match point, or you are ahead a set and two breaks and then fail to win a game the rest of the match, or you make 6 unforced errors in a row when tied at 5-5 in the match that will determine whether your team wins the league, etc. Clearly the fault is mental! But… I believe…

Most unforced errors are not due to mental errors
AND
Most lost matches to inferior players are not due to mental errors,
but are actually due to lack of muscle memory

Unforced errors are the result of one (or a combination) of three things:

- Your opponent hit a damn good shot. Give him/her credit! (Maybe they read this book!)
- Mental errors
- Muscle memory deficits

It is a fact that mental errors and lapses occur and cause one to lose on occasions. The Mental aspect is critically important and can give you the edge over your opponents. There are many promotional books, web sites, and training programs, sports psychologists, etc. to promote the development of mental aspect of playing tennis, and other sports. They also claim wonderful results and improvement in confidence, attention, focus, etc. Just search the web. There are many books on the subject, especially as related to tennis. I fully acknowledge that they help millions of tennis players the world over! I believe the mental aspect of the game is critically important!

No one truly knows if any one unforced error is 10% or 90% due to mental errors or the lack of muscle memory. Such a discussion wastes time and energy. Note that a significant portion of this book is devoted to the mental aspect, in this case "Imagery".

Moving On!

Instead, I believe the two work beautifully together – the mental game and the acquiring of tennis skills via Muscle Memory Practice. The mental game trains, hones, and augments your skills and match play. But my book primarily targets Muscle Memory Practice to physically obtain the skills development through acquisition and consolidation. My focus is on building muscle memory, and improving your game – through Muscle Memory Practice.

So, please allow me to develop this thought (and then to meld it together with the mental game).

My point is that many match losses are
primarily due to lack of muscle memory,
rather than not "having your head together"

Here is the mathematical support for this proposal. First, note that unforced errors, and/or lack of "good shots", can cause you to lose your match to an inferior player, or one of equal ability. Many (no one knows what percent) of your poor shots are simply lack of good muscle memory.

To understand this, go back to "The Sven Simulator" chapter. Let's say you really are better than your opponent, but not by much. Suppose that EVERY time you lose, you blame your lack of confidence, lapses in attention, lack of focus, etc. But what do the numbers tell you?

As noted, you are better than your opponent but not by much. Say you win 51% of 100 points. The simulator shows that out of 100 matches, you will win about 60% or your matches. Interesting, but we have already established that. Now, remember this chapter title is "It Isn't All Mental". To understand this, you need to go back to the table of 100 matches when you win 51% of the points. Let's take the numbers 59-41 as an average representation (meaning out of 100 matches, you win 59 and your opponent wins 41).

(Cue – this is where you turn back a few pages and look at the table.)

Review some of the losing scores. Now note the lopsided score in some of the matches. For example, using the sample table in the preceding chapter, note some of the losing scores by the better player:

Match #11 is 1-6, 0-6

Match #22 is 2-6, 3-6

Match #33 is 1-6, 4-6

Match #70 is 4-6, 2-6

Match #74 is 1-6, 2-6

Match #86 is 6-7, 1-6

Match #96 is 2-6, 3-6.

Sounds bad? Real bad!!! I am sure you would normally blame yourself, and then beat yourself up. But was it really a bad day mentally? Statistically not – It is just the reality of a statistical fact, a mathematical probability. It is going to happen; you might as well accept it.

Now let's continue. You are playing against a weaker opponent, winning 6 out of 10 matches. Note in matches 29-33 – you lose 5 matches in a row, and from 26-33 you lost 7 out of 8 – all to a player that you usually win about 60% of the time (meaning you win 51% out of 100 points). Again, sounds like a really bad mental slump, doesn't it?

But it is not! To restate: It is purely the reality of a statistical fact, a mathematical probability. The fact is that overall you win 51% of the points, and win most matches. But because you ONLY win 51% of the points, you WILL sometimes lose by these scores, and this many games in a row. These are mathematical facts based on statistical probability outcomes. Numbers do not have opinions, people do. That's why when you lose 1-6, 0-6; 2-6, 3-6; or 6-7, 1-6, you explain it away as a bad day mentally. But, statistically, the numbers and probability show that it <u>may</u> be entirely due to the fact that you only win 51% of your points. Yes, it could still be mental, but then again, it could be a real statistical probability outcome (no one can say for sure). Whether the cause is mental or physical, you will have days like that. And if you were to improve your skills just incrementally, then you would have fewer of them.

So quit beating yourself up for a lack of mental focus, when actually the problem may be that you've never established the degree of muscle memory that you need. To blame yourself for failing mentally (as a result of lack of confidence, inattention, lack of focus, etc.) accomplishes little, if anything.

So what to do? What can you do to fix this situation? What can be done to achieve Better Tennis? First, and foremost, give your opponent some credit. Next, ask whether you did the right things mentally (I defer to the many other experts on this). Then, do an honest analysis of what happened, and what you can do about it.

Accept the fact that you played reasonably well, given the limits of your game (think muscle memory). Deal with the fact you need to hit better shots and fewer unforced errors. Next, move forward to try to remedy the situation. That is, you need to improve your good shots via Muscle Memory Practice. Accept that you are only 51% better than your opponent. Accept that, objectively, if you are only better by 2 points out of 100, then you will occasionally lose big, and may also lose several games in a row.

The mathematical facts are: You lost by this frequency and this margin because these are the "Laws of Probability" and outcomes. This is a good example of the fact that you may not be having mental lapses. It may not be your mental game that is causing you to lose.

Moving On!

Remember that good muscle memory is the automatic unconscious reaction that makes you hit the ball the way you want. To succeed, you must improve the muscle memory associated with good tennis strokes.

Understand that by performing Muscle Memory Practice, you are working to improve that weak backhand, strengthening your forehand, sharpening up your volleys, etc. You will get better! Now, by making the commitment to Muscle Memory Practice, and practicing the physical aspect of the game for the next 3 weeks, only on a single shot, you can have a real chance of increasing your winning percentage of points to at least 54%. Now when you run the simulations for that, you win about 80 to 90% of your matches, instead of about 60%. Now, when you lose, it is really close, and you do not lose multiple matches in a row. This is all due to muscle memory. You did not work at all on your mental aspect of the game, but your poor shots are way down! You are winning the critical points!

What happens mentally? Now there is an added bonus. Even though you did not work at all on the mental aspect of your game, nevertheless, the mental game is much improved! Your confidence in your backhand, or the strength of your forehand, is way up. The anxiety is down; the calmness is there. The focus is there. The Get Set with the focus on doing a Head Turn and seeing the ball is there. All of these are "mental" (anticipatory) aspects of the game. They are all improved simply because you built your muscle memory. Remember the very definition of "Muscle Memory" which states that "Muscle Memory involves consolidating a specific motor task into memory through repetition. When a movement is repeated over time, a long-term muscle memory is created for that task, eventually allowing it to be performed without conscious effort. This process decreases the need for attention and creates maximum efficiency within the motor and memory systems" ("Muscle Memory", 2017, para 1).

Like improving at any sport or skill, it does take some effort on your part. But this method can optimize that effort in the most efficient way. With sequential sessions of Muscle Memory Practice in a concentrated period of time, your effort can make your game better for months or years. It is all about building muscle memory, and this ties in beautifully with augmenting your mental game.

By concentrated effort on physically developing your shots through Muscle Memory Practice, your mental game also improves. Success will come. It is a virtuous cycle. As your physical skills improve, your confidence, calm, focus, and motivation improves, then your practice improves, then that reinforces your muscle memory, then your game improves in skill and consistency, then your confidence, calm, focus, and motivation all improve further . . . repeat! Nice!

Notes

- The top players emphasize the importance of the mental game. They are right! They have the confidence, focus, etc. that enables them to succeed. However, they also hit better than the 99.99 . . . % of other players. So it is not all mental. If it were, then all the players with huge egos and tremendous self-confidence, would win and be in the top ranks. If it were all mental, then a player ranked at #100-200 with ego and confidence would be in the top ten! The pros have the mental game, but they also have developed their muscle memory to permit the physical and mental components to merge. They've got it together mentally, but they've also got the game – their shot-making ability, their points won, etc. The pros work extremely hard. They have spent thousands of hours developing their strokes – their muscle memory. Their muscle memory is what makes their game work. Simply put, they hit better! Their hard work and their great shots give them confidence. You have to have confidence and other mental skills to play at your best, but all this is fused with their muscle memory too. In summary: It isn't all mental, and it isn't all muscle memory either – IT IS BOTH.
- Let me state also the obvious: There is a very strong genetic component to all this (Duh)! So, as the saying goes: "Choose your parents well"!
- Note, however, that if you did not choose your parents based on athletic prowess, you at least have this book to help.
- Strategy is really important, so go buy a book on that.
- This is all theory and based my beliefs, common sense, some science, and a bit of experience.
- See Caveat #10 and the rest of the Caveats.

Chapter 23: Don't Let the Perfect Be the Enemy of the Good

I have repeatedly stated that 3 weeks of Muscle Memory Practice is the optimal period of time required to truly consolidate your muscle memory. This seems to be what is needed, in the strictly scientific sense, for long-lasting consolidation of the newly acquired or refined motor actions to occur. This is the time period needed for the brain to physically and functionally undergo change.

As an adult, it really is difficult to do 3 weeks of at least every other day practicing. Acknowledged! But you can make significant improvements quickly by just going 3 to 5 sessions in one week – just ONE week!!! I believe that you will be truly amazed at how much you can progress (if you use Muscle Memory Practice) in a relatively short period of time. If you are just picking up the sport, your gain will be even greater. But if you have been playing for years, then it will take longer to make new muscle memories that will become the preferred pathways. However, either way, it really does not matter. If you want improvement, then just give it 4 to 5 sessions in one week. If you want the improved game to really stay with you substantially longer, then add more time.

Some more detail: So 3 weeks is ideal. But be mindful that this is a generalization. Generalizations apply to large groups. Individuals vary. What is needed for each person will vary. For example, a person who has only recently started the game may only need 4 sessions in one week to result in a 20% to 30% improvement. However, a player who has been a 3.5, 4.0, or 4.5 player for 10 years (and remains at the same level despite taking lots of lessons, going to clinics, playing three to four times per week, etc.) may need longer than one week to develop new skills, or to refine existing skills. For that player, the development of new muscle memory paths will have to compete with established memory paths that have been used for 10 years, so it will take longer than 4 to 5 sessions. But if you can string together several sessions of Muscle Memory Practice in a short period of time, you will see improvement. For these experienced players, who have been playing for many years, it will take a few extra sessions to create the new muscle memory path and learn to train themselves to use the new path during match play (because that old Memory path is totally ingrained, established, and preferred).

However, I very strongly believe that with just a few sessions of Muscle Memory Practice, you will see meaningful improvements in your tennis game. I doubt your tennis friends will notice a 3% difference. After all, that just means you only win three more points out of 100. But you will notice you are winning more (see Sven simulator chapter).

If you stay with Muscle Memory Practice for another 1 to 2 weeks, you may get to the 5 to 10% (maybe even 20% plus) level of improvement (and I really believe you will). Then others will start to notice.

Confession – I know 3 weeks of at least every other day would be optimal (I have never done it), but do not obsess over that. I think I have practiced 6 times over about two weeks on maybe two occasions. I have completed 5 times of every other day a few times (although there were also times in the following month that I practiced the same stroke 3 to 4 times in a week).

Nevertheless, in spite of my genetic material, age, etc., I have definitely improved at a faster rate than ANY of the "old" practice routines I had tried – and it stayed with me longer.

Practice smart if practice time is limited. Using the principles of Muscle Memory Theory, learn to practice smart. Previously, I looked like I was working really hard when I practiced once per week (against the ball machine) for several weeks. Actually, that is true. I was working hard. However, I was not making any progress. But I wised up. Now I rarely practice if I can only go out once a week against the ball machine (instead I do a clinic-type workout). But when I am trying to improve, I will practice at least 4 times within one week. Now I continue to make progress when I commit to at least 4 times in one week, even if it is once every 2 to 3 months. When I do this, the improvement is greater and stays with me longer.

However, the science says 3 weeks (of every day, or at least every other) is best – but less helps too. Here is my best guess summary for practicing daily (or close to it):

- Around 1 week – one stroke, practice nothing after that practice session, do not practice any other motor skill afterward – you know – Muscle Memory Practice. The improvements may last a few weeks.
- Around 1½ to 2 weeks, the improvement lasts several weeks or months, longer if you repeat a similar practice session again the next month.
- Around 2 weeks, it lasts months, and very probably longer
- Around 3 weeks, it lasts years
- Around 4 weeks – you've "nailed it"!
- Go 3 to 4 sessions in a week – then repeat in a month, then next month. Your muscle memory "learns" faster – you do retain more muscle memory with each group of practice sessions. It starts to add up!

So shoot for the ideal, but accept what you can do. Obviously, if you go three times a week (and not every other day) for 2 weeks, then this will help some. However, from experience, I think at least every other day is better than 3 times in one week.

Bottom line – You say you want to play Better Tennis, but if you can't find time for one short week of Muscle Memory Practice, then you are kidding yourself!

So shoot for the ideal, but accept what you can do!

Notes

- Every other day for 4 times in one week is far better than once per week for a month.
- Reminder – This is what defines Muscle Memory Practice:
  - Deliberate practice
  - Singular focused practice of on one specific skill (for example, a cross-court forehand – not a cross-court and a down the line)

- Repetition is in a concentrated period of time (daily or at least every other day practice extending at least 5 to 7 sessions)
- Requires that no other types of practice occupy your practice session. It is especially important to not practice any other type of stroke, or other motor skill, at the end of your practice session.
- Remember, the last motor skill you work on is the most likely to undergo consolidation (that is, to become incorporated into your long-term muscle memory).
- Important point of clarification: I have repeatedly used the time-period of 3 weeks as an optimal duration to achieve long term retention of newly learned or refined motor skills. It is. However (stating the obvious), this does not mean you develop a perfect forehand (or whatever stroke) in 3 weeks. Nevertheless, the degree of improvement, although limited, will be substantial. Hopefully, you will have an accelerated path of improvement and long-term retention, more than at any other time in your life. Still, let's be realistic.

Chapter 24: About Me

My tennis story is this – I have not played a lifetime of tennis. I played two years at my small town high school. Then for the next 10 years or so, I played a friend here or there, maybe a half-dozen times a year. Then I did not play for decades. I started playing more regularly about 10 years ago, but still was working full-time and busy with my family.

Also, I am not the best natural athlete, to put it mildly! I am skinny, short, weak, and slow. My reflexes are definitely slower than normal. My hand-eye coordination is well below average – and now I am old (65 years old at the time of first writing this book).

Sounds kind of bad, but it is worse than that – so let me put all this in more proper perspective. I grew up in a small east Texas town. My high school graduating class was around 100. All the way from elementary through senior in high school, we had PE (physical education). When we ran races, I was the slowest in the entire class. When teams were chosen, I was almost always last (and this in spite of being relatively popular).

I am exactly the opposite of a "natural athlete". That is just how it is.

However, I have had recent success in tennis. A few years ago, in my early 60s, I was a mid-level 3.5. I noticed my game slipping, even though I was playing about 3 times per week, going to clinics, and hitting occasionally against the ball machine. I figured that is just how things are when you get older. I then came up with, and partially started implementing, my Muscle Memory theory and Practice. I guess I am lucky (in retrospect) to not be a natural athlete, because I have had to come up with props, prompts, and practice methods to compensate for my lack of athletic ability.

Instead of getting worse, I started getting better. To be honest, until last year, I never did more than a few days of Muscle Memory Practice in a one-week period (which is why I have since written my "How To" chapters – see later in the book). Nevertheless, instead of getting worse, I started to improve.

Last year I won the 3.5 Men's division of the long running main City of Austin tournament – the Courtyard Classic – in singles. I beat a 26 year old in the finals. Now I am being recruited by different USTA teams that win regional and go to Sectionals, but cannot quite break through. They think I could be the answer (I am not convinced, but I surely take it as a compliment). Now I play #1 doubles for my Austin Tennis League (never happened previously). Now I get recruited to be a doubles partner in the final Texas tournament where only the top 8 teams (for that division) are selected to compete. Now I can hit comfortably with and against 4.0 and 4.5 men – maybe not "too comfortably" with the 4.5 guys. (Yes, the 4.5 guys are tough – but I hang in there pretty well.) I also now routinely play with or against players who were college scholarship Division 1A athletes who have been playing tennis for years. That is quite remarkable, practically impossible, for the loser of the PE class.

This only means – given the genetic material I was born with, and given the limited amount of time that I have had to work on my game, and given that I have never fully committed to my

Muscle Memory Practice, and considering my OLD AGE – that I clearly have gotten better, while most others have not.

I feel safe in saying that many who are my age do not play as well as they did when they were younger. Furthermore, I have improved rather efficiently, and with only an abbreviated form of Muscle Memory Practice. I find it fantastic that I have improved significantly. I am in my mid-60s and not really spending that much time on the courts, but I am improving.

Also consider that I am skinny, small, short, weak, slow, somewhat poorly coordinated, have slower than normal reflexes…and now am OLD (age 65 at the writing of this book, actually closer to age 66). However, I clearly have gotten better every time I used Muscle Memory Practice for around a week – even with just an hour a day over 5 times!

I conclude there may be something to my theory.

More confessions

I am embarrassed that I have not (YET!) completed my full 3 weeks session related to fully developing Muscle Memory. I am hesitant to confess this, but I am very honest. I do not want to deceive or mislead.

Also, I really am a busy person. The courts are always booked at nights and on weekends. I admit it is difficult. There are all kinds of good excuses to not "Get it Done". In my journey to Better Tennis I picked up quite a bit of experience. I can confidently say that just hitting against a ball machine or with a pro is not going to take you very far if it's done in the usual random manner. As you now know, I have carefully thought about this and reviewed the subject. Hence, Muscle Memory Theory and Practice.

Thankfully, even a smattering of Muscle Memory Practice can get meaningful results. Think about all the disadvantages that I have, and that I never fully applied my theories, but I have clearly gotten significantly better. I am in the bottom 5% of athletic ability. Think of the possibilities for improvement to the other 95% of you! Consider what this means to someone who is younger than age 65. Contemplate what this would do for your game if you are willing to commit to just a few weeks of the needed effort that is Muscle Memory Practice.

We are what we are. I get it. But if I can become a dominant 3.5 (or a decent 4.0 player), then think what someone with youth and natural gifts could accomplish. Me, I'm 65. I was going downhill, but I have now improved. Think what you can do! It is safe to say that, most of you, with your size, speed, reflexes, coordination, youth, etc. – that you can do so much better. Heck, just think if you actually completed the recommended 3 weeks of Muscle Memory Practice!

I have really tried hard to write something that will be helpful. So now we move on to another topic. I clearly recognize that getting 3 weeks of at least every other day practice has many significance obstacles. All of us have many distractions (busy life, booked courts, weather, etc.) to overcome. That is why I have recently researched and added another chapter to this book, the Chapter on "How To". Read on!

Chapter 25: How to Get It Done!
For Muscle Memory Practice

"Success is a few simple disciplines, practiced every day"
Jim Rohn
(Quote of the Day Show)

I admit that it is not easy to commit yourself to daily, or every-other-day, practice for at least a week or two (preferably three). However, doing it is even more difficult. I had difficulty doing it. Between a very busy irregular work schedule, a very involved family life, booked tennis courts almost every night and weekends, it is hard. So what to do?

As noted, if you cannot practice every week, then go 3 to 4 times for one week. Then repeat 2 weeks later. Although some will be lost, you will progress. Similarly, if you practice 3 to 4 times for 1 week and repeat 4 weeks later, you will also progress. (Remember also that according to the Laws of Muscle Memory, you will progress faster if you practice 4 times in one week than once per week for a month). Do this just a few times; it really starts to add up. Of course, more is better, and per Muscle Memory theory, 3 weeks of at least every other is definitely optimal. It is the focused training in a concentrated period of time that establishes the muscle memory.

Now, back to how to get yourself to complete this focused training. Here are some tips. First, some motivational inspiration:

"Nothing can substitute for just plain hard work"
Andre Agassi
(Brainy Quote)

"There is no way around hard work. Embrace it.
You have to put in the hours because there is always something you can improve.
You have to put in a lot of sacrifice and effort for sometimes little reward
but you have to know that, if you put in the right effort,
the reward will come"
Roger Federer
(AZ Quotes)

OK – now you are good to go! All fixed and solved now! That was not hard, was it?

Well actually that did not work for me either! Maybe some more is needed? I reviewed and read quite a bit on this, because I was not "Getting It Done". In my review, my favorites were "The Power of Habit", and especially the writings of James Clear. His writings are AWESOME.

They both focus on establishing life-long habits, or at least habits of long duration. James Clear calls it "Habit Formation". His site and writings are great! Thoughtful and well researched. It is also free. I would highly recommend reading what he writes (See James Clear – james@jamesclear.com), and subscribing to his free weekly newsletter.

However, none of this addressed our specific need. What we need here is a method to successfully complete a 3-week focused project – in this case, Muscle Memory Practice, and a "never fail" habit formation for only 3 weeks (although if you can do this for just 1 to 2 weeks, then I think your tennis will be noticeably better).

This sort of thing comes up in life: That is, the need for a focused effort for a limited period of time. For students, it is a term paper, or a thesis. For working adults, it is a business project, or training session. For amateur athletes, it is a focused dedicated effort to make a lot of improvement in the shortest period of time. Hopefully, in the most efficient, focused manner, with the maximal long term positive effect – such as my theory of Muscle Memory Practice and its application to tennis.

So here is my own version. Many of the principles are similar to what is already established for the development of long range habit development, but I adapted them to Muscle Memory Practice for Better Tennis. This is a suggested plan (to be honest – another unproven theory – see Caveat #10) for a 3-week focused effort to improve your tennis game. This is how to "Get It Done".

Step #1 – Write it down using a Commitment Contract

A Commitment Contract is a binding agreement you sign with yourself to ensure that you follow through with your intentions – and it does this by utilizing the psychological power of loss aversion and accountability to drive behavior change. It is a contract with yourself! It is a commitment!

You sign it, in front of witnesses – that would be your tennis gang (note I just said witnesses – I did not stipulate high moral character, etc.). These are your enforcers – the judge, jury, and executioner to hold you accountable to your written contract.

Committing your goals in writing and confirming them with others is a powerful way to ensure you stick to your goal. Make it hard to fail, but easy to succeed. Make a penalty and a reward (Fitzpatrick, 2010). This can really help. We all respond to carrots and sticks. The stick can be something as simple as the disappointment and shame you feel among your tennis gang, and the carrot can be something as simple as pizza and beer for success. You write down what you will do, and when you will do it, and where. This is your commitment – a contract with yourself witnessed by others. It will be a schedule for your practice. You are not listing goals, you are listing the plan of action.

Another version of this is called an "Implementation Intention". An implementation intention is when you state your intention to implement a particular behavior at a specific time in the future. Fact: By completing this simple sentence, you are 2x - 3x more likely to succeed related to exercise, and I would think most other plans. So complete this sentence:

"During the next week, I will partake in at least 20 minutes of vigorous exercise on [Day] at [Time of Day] at/in [Place]"
(Milne, Orbell, & Sheeran, 2002, page 170)

A few more details on this because it is really significant. The study was trying to get people to exercise. Both groups read an educational leaflet about heart disease and the benefits of exercise. It even talked about the possible painful and debilitating effects of heart disease. The exercise rate for that group was 35%. However, when another group read the same leaflet, and completed the above statement, the exercise rate went to 91%.

Similar findings have been found to occur across many studies. That is, writing down your plan significantly increases the odds of successfully completing that plan. Wow!

So Get It Done! Set a schedule for your actions. Once you know what you want, the schedule defines doing it. Set a schedule for your Muscle Memory Practice by using the Commitment Contract and Implementation Intention statements.

Now take it further. Note that a good plan also anticipates problems. Accept that it is not easy to put forth additional energy and effort. So many distractions come up in day-to-day life. It is easy to get side-tracked. What to do? The answer is to add further to your written plan (that would be your contract).

You do this by adding a "Distraction Plan" for Muscle Memory Practice. This is a list of all the things that might cause a distraction. Anticipate the obstacles. Now eliminate your distractions. You need time for your planned practice sessions. That also means something needs to be eliminated. So also decide what to eliminate over the next week (or 3 weeks), because there are so many distractions. Plan it. Write it down. Remove the distractions.

Be detailed on your plan to counter unplanned distractions. Then think of ways to prevent them from happening. Ask yourself questions like:

- What do I do if I just don't feel like it?
- What if I get off work late?
- What if it rains?

How do you plan to work around these problems – these distractions?? How do you get back on track? Remember, you need to persist, to continue. You do not need to be perfect.

Once you have finalized your schedule, and your plan for possible distractions, read the written copy every night before bed. Also, have a copy of it on your phone so that you have to read it when your alarm goes off (see below).

Step #2 – Get Started

"Attempts fail, but not as certainly as tasks never attempted"
Unknown

You have to start (Duh)! You have to show up! The hardest step is the first one. The first steps are the most important.

Just show up! Consistently getting on the court is what you must strive for. Let's just say you do not feel like practice that day. That's OK – so only doing 15 minutes is OK. But you have to convince yourself that YOU MUST DO AT LEAST 15 MINUTES (daily or at least every other day). If you practice for 15 minutes, but then do not feel like it, then at least you tried. It is acceptable. But there are few excuses that are acceptable for not putting forth 15 minutes of effort.

Your action speaks the clearest. You must consistently take action. Simply put, you must at least get on the court and get started.

Make it easy to get started. Make it so that no excuse is acceptable. Start with small steps – say a 15-minute practice as a minimum. I'm not asking for much – just 15 minutes on the court is what you must do. There is hardly any excuse that works to prevent that! Structure everything to make your Muscle Memory Practice more likely. Make the initial tasks so easy that you do it without having to force yourself.

Step #3 – Minimize

Think about the minimum amounts of work that must happen. In order to "Get It Done", you need to ignore some other things. Schedule your time on the tennis courts as far in advance as you can. Schedule for the entire week.

Some suggestions:

- The day before the first practice, gather your tennis clothes, shoes, bag, and racket as soon as you get home. You just made it so much easier to practice the next day. Then immediately put it all in your car. Now you have nothing to deal with the next morning because you have already gotten started. You have minimized your effort to start. If you can do these simple tasks (total time less than two minutes), then your odds of going out and practicing increase dramatically. These tasks are so easy, you can't say no to them. Then follow the same routine every time.
- When you finish work, do not go home (way too many distraction there!). You already have your tennis clothes, shoes, bag, and racket in the car. So now drive straight to the courts. Again, make it easy to get started.

Note if you go to practice tennis immediately after work, that means you have to eliminate some of your routine things for that week/month. It means you will not be watching the news and having a glass of wine or a beer at 5:30. That means you may need to record the news and watch at 7:00 instead of 5:30. That means your significant other needs to be part of this change in your schedule for the next 3 weeks. It may also mean that you will not be having mid-week matches for 1 to 3 weeks.

Now, stick to your schedule for one week. Just follow it for this week. For the next 7 days, don't let distractions get in the way. Get some momentum. Always show up. Successful tennis players find a way to practice – no matter what. They get results because they show up – despite the distractions. They do not accept excuses. Embrace the process and stay with it! After all, for now you are "Getting it Done" for only one week. Get that first week accomplished no matter what happens!

"You have to believe in the long term plan you have but you need the short term goals to motivate and inspire you"
Roger Federer
(January 28, 2017, Fearless Motivation – Quote #10)

Then commit to another week (although you know that you really are planning for a full 3 weeks of at least every other day practice). However, note that once you have gotten started, you now have momentum. You have committed to the process. You must follow your plan. NO excuses (reread the above paragraph).

"There are only results, anything else is just an excuse"
Unknown

You do not think about it – you just "Do it"!

If you are to be successful, then you will stay with the plan, the contract, that you committed to. After all, it is only for 3 weeks. Think about it. 3 weeks of hard work, but your tennis game should show a noticeable improvement and stay with you for a really long time (per Muscle Memory Practice theory). This should be well worth the effort.

Some days you may not feel like it, but you have already strategized. Use your plan to overcome it (see "Distraction Plan"). If you are able to plow through it for this short 3 weeks, then all should be better. Be successful – Successful players Get it Done! They show up and do their practice.

"It's the ability to work when work isn't easy that makes the difference…
If you look at the people who are consistently achieving their goals,
you start to realize that it's not the events or the results that make them different.
It's their commitment to the process"
James Clear
(2013, September 19, from section "Working when work isn't easy" and "It's not the event, it's the process")

After all, it is only 3 weeks.

Step #4 – Use a Visual Cue

A visual cue is a reminder of both what you need to do, and what you have already accomplished. If you are successful, it provides concrete evidence that you are moving in the right direction. It shows your progress towards successfully implementing you plan. It is proof of your progress. It rewards your success. It also reminds you to continue future work that is needed to fulfill your "contract". It adds motivation to continue to build your current momentum. Bottom line – it can help a lot, so USE IT!!!

So how do you do that? Simply place three $1 bills in a clear glass or jar after every Muscle Memory Practice. One look at your jar full of money and you immediately have a measure of your progress. Visual cues serve to motivate you further creating a virtuous cycle. As the visual evidence of your progress mounts, you become more motivated to continue. The more money you place in the bin, the more motivated you will become to finish the task. Watch it accumulate! When you have completed your 3 weeks of at least every other day practice, have a party for your tennis friends.

Summary – Write it down – Commit and schedule!

* Sign a commitment contract, including the use of an implementation intention statement. Complete the sentences: "During the next week, I will partake in at least _____ (fill in the blank) minutes of Muscle Memory Practice on [Day] at [Time of Day] at/in [Place]". (This is "Your Plan", "Your schedule" — It is critically important!!!)

* Write your Distraction Plan.

* Start (make it easy to start) – then No Excuses!

* Minimize – Gather your tennis clothes, shoes, bag, and racket together and place all of this in your car the night before. After work the next day, drive straight to the courts.

* Use a visual cue – Place three $1 bills in a clear glass or jar after every Muscle Memory deliberate practice.

Notes

* More on the Tennis Log that I emphasized in an earlier chapter. Keep a tennis log and record your progress to see how far you have come. This is important so that you realize how much you have achieved. You should do this by keeping a notebook where you specifically record how much progress is made. You should also record any little bits of information you discovered that improve your play. Do this after practice sessions and matches.

* Maybe use your apps. Think about this as a "Commitment Device". Consider setting your phone alarm to sound three hours, one hour, and minutes before your planned workout. This psyches you up. Develop steps that make it easy to perform your Muscle Memory Practice, so you can increase your consistency, and ultimately your Getting It Done.

* Ask a friend (or friends) for help. We all need help. Get a family member or tennis friend(s) to ask about your progress. Let them know they need to give you a hard time if you do not stick with your schedule. After all, they are invested in your success, as there will be no free beer and pizza if you fail!

Chapter 26: Stuck

Being stuck is bad! It even sounds like a bad word.

I ask you – Are you stuck? Are you in the same place that you have been for the last 2 to 3 years. The same place on the club tennis ladder, or the city tennis league? Or the same state ranking? The same national ranking? The same world ranking? Oh, you might move up or down a few minor positions, but be honest – are you really moving up? Getting better?

Sure, you have had lessons, clinics, camps, and practice sessions. But if you are a club player, are you still in the middle of the pack? Are you still "just" a 3.5 or 4.0 or whatever – even after all these years of trying – hoping – to get better and move up? Tired of being stuck?

If you are a world class player (you may even have had your own coaches, or perhaps series of coaches), are you still stuck in the bottom half of the top 100 – for years?! Well do something about it! Be radical! Really change what you do – how you practice.

Remember the quote,

> *"Insanity is doing the same thing over and over and expecting different results"*
> Unknown (Quote Investigator – attributed to Einstein but no proof of that)

So if you want different results, then you have to actually do something different!

That would be to max out on Muscle Memory Practice. Hit nothing but your cross-court forehand (or backhand down the line – whatever) – in all your practice sessions. Repeat thousands of times, even after you hit it well. This is critically important!

Remember the principles of Muscle Memory Practice:

- You do deliberate practice. You challenge yourself. You strive for what you cannot consistently perform. Focus to make every repetition better
- You focus on only one aspect of one shot – say the cross-court forehand (not the forehand down the line)
- You do not – no matter what – practice or hit another shot after your practice session.
- You do this at least every other day for 3 weeks. Your pro observes and helps you focus relentlessly on the proper technique (especially the Keystone Habits – Get Set, Head Turn and Sweet Spot – including use of Tai Chi strokes).
- You have really worked on your one shot (say the cross-court forehand) and are consistently doing it well – REMEMBER – this is when the "work" really starts. This is when you need to keep doing the same shot (or pattern) for another 2 to 3 weeks – nothing else.

As I have said before:

Don't practice until you hit it right,
Practice until you can't hit it wrong
Anonymous

Be a purist! Do not be afraid to commit to working on just one shot. After all – what do you have to lose? You are already stuck. You ain't getting better. You need to do something radical to break out. At the very worst, your other shots may fall off some (but then they may not – in fact they could get better – especially if you have been working on your Fundamentals, the Keystone Habits).

We are talking about the potential of significantly improving your game forever! So what is the risk vs. benefit ratio? How does the potential risk stack up against the potential gain?

So you can maybe move forward, or you can stay stuck!

Section II: Imagery

It Works

Really!!!

Chapter 27: Imagery Definitions

Imagery – "to create an experience in the mind" (I shortened the definition used by Weinberg, 2008, p. 1). The goal of imagery is using your mind or imagination to see and feel yourself playing the point, as if you are actually there. It is seeing and doing what you normally see and do if you are playing the point. It is as if a real life experience is happening to you. You are practicing, or perhaps better termed, mentally rehearsing, your shots. In fact, some even call it "mental rehearsal". It also goes by the term "visualization". Imagery helps you perform the shots you need when you need them.

There are many kinds of imagery – visual, kinesthetic, auditory, smell, etc. The two most common, and relevant to tennis, are visual and kinesthetic.

Visual – You see, in your mind, as if you are actually there. Visual is divided into two categories – Internal and External.

Internal visual imagery is where you imagine being inside your own body. It is the first person perspective. You are seeing images as through your own eyes. You see the ball leave the opponents racket and coming toward you. You imagine, or visualize, what you see when you play points as if through your own eyes.

External visual imagery is viewing from the perspective of an observer, as if watching TV, film, video, or movie. It is as if someone did a videotape of you playing. It is the third person perspective. This is what an observer would see watching you play points.

Kinesthetic imagery is when you feel as if your own body is doing it. You imagine being inside your own body. You are experiencing playing the actual point in tennis play. You feel as if your body is performing the movement. You feel your legs as you run toward the ball. You feel your arms as you hit the stroke. Your feel yourself use your arms and legs to Get Set, you feel your Head Turn to watch the ball, you feel the ball strike the Sweet Spot of the racket. You internalize the feel of the movement as if your body is actually performing the movement. For advanced athletes, this is used most often.

Chapter 28: Internal vs External

So which is better? This has been reviewed by multiple researchers. Unfortunately, there are conflicting results as to which format of imagery helps the most, depending on what type of athletic sport, and on differing levels of athletic expertise. I will list some publications results below, but for now I will give you my personal take.

The most useful form of imaging (internal visual, external visual, kinesthetic) is probably dependent on the stage of learning. In the early stage, early learning, the external perspective seems to be most beneficial. For later stages, the internal is probably better. Also, the kinesthetic is likely most helpful to the skilled athlete, especially when combined with an internal perspective.

I recommend using them all. We are all different, so what works best for one may not work best for another. Therefore, test all three. Test in a variety of different scenarios and game situations. What works best in one scenario may not necessarily work best in another. Mentally practice your strokes. Mentally play points in your mind. Determine what works best for you, and in what situation it seems to work.

By now, you know Muscle Memory Practice. Since there is a correlation on a neurophysiological basis (read next chapter) between imagery and actual performance, utilize the Muscle Memory Practice principles and apply them to Imagery. Program and reprogram your mind and muscles utilizing Imagery until the neural pathways are formed.

As noted above, there are several published reports related to the use of different imagery perspectives – internal visual, external visual, and kinesthetic. Here are a few significant ones:

- White and Hardy (1995, p. 169) noted "Internal visual imagery was more effective for the planning of action in response to changes in a visual field" and that "external visual imagery was found to be more effective for both learning and subsequent retention".

- "Kinesthetic imagery ability scores correctly classified a majority of the subjects as medalists versus non-medalists" (Vadoa, Hall, & Moritz, 1997, p. 241).

- "Athletes at the highest level, most use internal visual imagery and kinesthetic imagery" (Nezam, IsaZedeh, Hojjati, & Zadeh, 2014. p. 712).

- Per another study, successful U.S. track and field athletes used more external imagery. Ungerleider and Golding (1991, p. 1016) note the "Olympians had a more external perspective in their imagery and there was a stronger physical sensation associated with that imagery than their non-Olympic colleagues" (on physical sensation, think kinesthetic).

- Hardy and Callow (1999) studied the use of internal visual imagery, external visual imagery, and kinesthetic imagery in three different groups (each group involving an entirely different set of motor skills, and with varying degrees of mastery in each group). More details on the groups follow: The first group consisted of accomplished karateists learning a new martial arts routine with 52 separate movements. The second group had 34 non-skilled participants learning a gymnastics routine. The third group used 20 expert rock climbers and a rock climbing challenge. They found that external visual imagery was significantly more effective than internal imagery in learning complex new motor skills in all groups. There was also a kinesthetic component to each group. In group one (the skilled karate group) and group three (the expert rock climbers), kinesthetic imagery helped. In group two (the non-skilled) participants, the kinesthetic imagery did not help. Bottom line: External imagery helps more than internal for tasks that are form dependent. Kinesthetic imagery is helpful, but you have to be at least somewhat skilled for the kinesthetic imagery to be beneficial. (A very nicely designed experiment, I think. This is a brief description. Please review the article for additional important details).

- In contrast, Rotella, Gansneder, Ojala, & Billing (1980) noted that better skiers focused on the difficult parts of the racecourse using an internal imagery perspective, and that the poorer performers used external perspective (third person view) when they were using their imagery.

- Mahoney and Avener (1977) noted Olympic team finalists reported using imagery extensively, but the better athletes reported a higher frequency of internal imagery rather than external imagery. They also noted that all the finalists said that they used imagery extensively.

- Abdin (2010) performed a comprehensive literature review related to imagery for past performance. He concluded that studies provide support in regards that internal imagery perspective correlates with enhanced performance on motor skill tasks.

- Murphy, Jowdy, & Durtschi published a study in 1989 (as cited in Nezam, IsaZadeh, Hojati, and Zadeh, 2014, p. 715) note that "For tasks that rely on kinesthetic awareness, [the reason] internal imagery has often been advocated and implemented as opposed to external imagery is because the internal perspective is presumed to have a stronger relationship to kinesthetic sensations".

Notes

- **Quick summary:** Visual external works best for beginners. Visual internal and kinesthetic works best for advanced, especially when combined. Intermediate should use all. Everyone is different, so try all. Use in a variety of different situations, as I suspect the best type of imagery could depend on the particular situation and your level of skill.

Chapter 29: Why Mental Imagery Works

To paraphrase Weinberg, 2008, p.1 – Studies indicate that the brain interprets highly vivid imagery as identical to the real situation.

The reason visual imagery works lies in the fact that when you imagine yourself performing to perfection, and doing precisely what you want, when you want to, you are in turn physiologically creating neural patterns in your brain, just as if you had physically performed the action. These pathways encode the brain with what you want to do, that is, the automaticity that comes with muscle memory. Porter notes (1990), "Hence, mental imagery is intended to train our minds and create the neural patterns in our brain to teach our muscles to do exactly what we want them to do" (as quoted in Plessinger, 2000, under subtopic "How Mental Imagery Works"). The odds that you are physically able to hit the necessary shot when you need to are increased because you have mentally practiced this stroke, this point, and this game scenario.

When you vividly see yourself playing a point, the brain utilizes some of the same pathways that are used when you perform the physical movements. We are training our brains, and even our muscles, to perform the desired strokes. We are executing the movement and the stroke itself perfectly. We are actually practicing the stroke through our Imagery, that is our mental rehearsal.

Although imagery obviously does not truly replicate the muscle movement, some of the paths are similar. But I also think there is something else. Somehow, the planning of the movement and the visualization, adds another dynamic. The duplication reinforces and adds to your muscle memory. It adds an element that is separate and apart from your usual physical practice. There are just too many studies that document this, so I believe it is a fact.

Taken together with your physical practice, the additional imagined neural patterns serve to reinforce and strengthen your game. The brain sees the imagery, your strokes, and the point you are imagining, as the real-life situation. There is further research to back this principle. The fact that imagery and motor movement are linked by similar brain connections and pathways is known as the principle of "functional equivalents" (Guillot, Genevois, Desliens, & Rogowski, 2012).

There is much research to show that motor imagery can significantly improve motor learning in motor performance.

Chapter 30: Why Use Imagery?

If you are a club player who wants to improve, to help your tennis team, to get revenge for that last painful loss, or simply to play better and enjoy this great sport more than you already do, then use imagery. It even helps pros! IT HELPS ALL!

See what some of the world's best athletes say:

"I really believe if you visualize yourself doing something,
you can make that image come true....
I must have rehearsed it ten thousand times.
And when it came true it was like an electric bolt went up my spine"
Wayne Gretzky
(retrieved from Weinberg, 2008, who cites, as quoted in Orlick, 1998, p. 67)

"I never hit a shot, not even in practice,
without having a very sharp in-focus picture of it in my head. It's like a color movie.
First I see the ball where I want it to finish, nice and white, sitting up high on bright green grass.
Then the scene quickly changes and I 'see' the ball going there; its path, trajectory and shape,
even its behavior on landing.
Then there is sort of a fade out, and the next scene shows me making the kind of swing
that will turn the images into reality on landing.
Finally, I see myself making the kind of swing that
that will turn the first two images into reality.
These 'home movies' are a key to my concentration"
Jack Nicklaus
(as quoted in AZ Quotes)

"I visualized where I wanted to be,
what kind of player I wanted to become.
I knew exactly where I wanted to go, and I focused on getting there"
Michael Jordon
(as quoted by Matthew Kelly, 1999)

Michael Phelps used Imagery. Phelps is the most decorated Olympian in history, with 23 Olympic gold medals and a total of 28 overall medals ("Michael Phelps", 2017, para. 1). His coach, Bob Bowman, would tell him do a mental visualization of the perfect race. The use of imagery was one of the essential components of his success. Read Charles Duhigg's excellent book on "The Power of Habit" for a fascinating and more detailed discussion of this.

A quote from his coach Bob Bowman (as noted in an interview by Amy Shipley and recorded in an article by Aimee Groth, 2012, para. 3 – in the Bibliography look under "Bowman, Bob"):

> *"He's the best I've ever seen — and he may be the best ever —*
> *in terms visualization", said Bowman.*
> *"He'll see [what he's up against] sitting in the stands,*
> *and then he'll see it in the water.*
> *And then he will go through scenarios – what if things, don't go well?"*
> Bob Bowman

Bottom line: Motor skills improve with use of imagery. This can be applied to all sports. This is especially true for tennis, as it is such a mental game. Further, imagery can help practically every aspect of your tennis game, including your muscle memory, strokes, serve, motivation, confidence, tactics, performance, and motor skills. It helps everything and it can help everyone, no matter what your tennis level – from novice to the top 10 pros. It helps ALL.

Notes

- Read Charles Duhigg's book on "The Power of Habit". It gives a wonderful inspiring more detailed account of how Michael Phelps and his coach used Imagery.

Chapter 31: General Studies to Support Imagery Use

The evidence is overwhelming. Practicing imagery helps PRACTICALLY EVERYTHING!

The Overall Summary

There is a large amount of evidence that supports this. In a review of psychological techniques, including Imagery, Mamassis and Doganis (2004, p. 118) say, "There have been many studies done in different sports dealing with both recreational (Efran, Lesser, & Spiller, 1994 [as cited in Mamassis and Doganis, 2004]) and competitive athletes (Patrick & Hrycaiko, 1998 [as cited in Mamassis and Doganis, 2004]). All of them showed a direct relationship between the use of one or a set of psychological techniques and improvement in performance". The best athletes and coaches utilize it.

It does not just improve one aspect of your game, it improves practically every aspect of your game:

- Mental preparation and performance
- Motor learning, including learning specific shots
- Accuracy and technical quality
- Confidence with belief you can succeed
- Managing arousal and anxiety before a match, and even changing the perception of that anxiety into something positive
- Positive thinking and setting higher goals
- Setting expectations with performance review and analysis
- Problem solving, including use of strategic thinking
- Adaptation to competitive matches and match stress
- Sticking to your planned training schedule (or increase your time spent doing what you hoped to do)
- Maintaining mental freshness during injury

This list is from research studies. These are the conclusions. Although the studies are from a variety of sports, not just tennis, I believe the principles still hold true.

The bullet points above are a summary testifying to the effectiveness of imagery related to sports. I tend to be a bit academic. I like references to substantiate "bullet points". In case you are also a bit academic, I have referenced the exact wording and sources of the bullet points in the sections below. Specifically, I cite the article that I reviewed. If there is a reference within the article, then I also cite that reference as I have done in the paragraph above titled "The Overall Summary").

Supporting Studies

- "There is now ample evidence that motor imagery contributes to enhanced motor performance" (Guillot, Desliens, Rouyer, & Rogowska, 2013, p. 332 in abstract).
- "A meta-analysis of the literature on mental practice was conducted to determine the effect of mental practice on performance and to identify conditions under which mental practice is most effective. Results indicated that mental practice has a positive and significant effect on performance" (Driskell, Copper, & Moran, 1994, p. 481 in abstract).
- "Being that Imagery has been shown to improve such key mental skills, in theory, the use of imagery should improve subsequent skill performance" (Abdin, 2010, p. 34).
- "Different uses of imagery in sport include: mental practice of specific performance skills, improving confidence and positive thinking, problem solving, controlling arousal and anxiety, performance review and analysis, preparation for performance, and maintaining mental freshness during injury" (Plessinger, 2000, para. 3).
- "To this end, it was found that 34 of the basketball players (94.44%) reported that the imagery training had led to improvements in their performance .... Of those players who indicated improvements to performance, 22 players (61.11%) reported specific improvements to skill technique and/or overall game play, 7 players (19.44%) reported improvements in concentration and focus, and 3 players reported improvements in confidence" (Cumming, Hall, Shambrook, 2004, p. 62).

Improved self-confidence and reduced anxiety

- Increased intensity of self-confidence
- Enhanced self-confidence
- Predicted self-confidence and self-efficacy (I define self-efficacy as 'belief in one's self')
- Controlled competitive anxiety
- Enhanced performance
- Turned anxiety into something positive

Supporting Studies

- "Examples of technical improvements included increases in skill technique and overall game play, while psychological improvements included enhancements in concentration and self-confidence". (Cumming, Hall, Shambrook, 2004, p. 66)
- "These results suggest that imagery can be used to help control competitive anxiety levels and enhance self-confidence". (Vadoa, Hall, & Moritz, 1997, p. 241).
- "Imagery was a significant predictor of self-confidence and self-efficacy in both recreational and competitive youth soccer players" (Munroe-Chandler, Hall, &Fishburne, 2008, p. 7). (Note – this was especially true related to Motivational General Mastery, which Weinberg (2008) defines as mastering a skill in a competitive situation.)
- "We also found that there is a high correlation between imagery and self-confidence" (Rattankoses, Omar-Frauzee, Geok, Abdullah, Choosakul, Nazaruddin, & Nordin, 2009, p. 138).

- "Results suggest that perceptions of anxiety may be modified by imagery, which could aid performance" (Page, Sime, & Nordell, 1999, p. 458).

- "Although there were no differences in physiological response intensities…these responses, along with anxiety symptoms, were interpreted as facilitative during the challenge script…Results support using imagery to facilitate adaptive stress appraisal" (Williams, Cumming, & Balanos, 2010, p. 339). Simply put, this means your match anxiety can be changed from a negative to a positive, from harmful to helpful, related to match results.

- "In the current study, elite athletes reported greater self-confidence and usage of imagery and self-talk than their non-elite counterparts…The findings of the current study provide the basis to indicate that certain psychological skills (i.e., imagery and self-talk) are implicated in helping elite performers maintain robust perceptions of confidence, in order to cope with the stressful demands of high-level competition" (Neil, Mellalieu, Hanton, 2006, pp. 420, 421).

Improved motivation
- Helps set realistic expectations
- Helps set higher goals
- Encourages more practice
- Encourages fulfilling training schedule (or improves effective use of time)

Supporting Studies
"Subjects in the performance imagery group spent significantly more time practicing the golf putting tasks than subjects in the control group. Subjects who use imagery also set higher goals for themselves, had more realistic self-expectations, and adhere more to their training programs outside of the laboratory" (Martin & Hall, C. R., 1995, p. 54). In other words, they were more motivated to practice.

Improved relaxation, skills and adaptation to stress
Use of imagery results in…

- Relaxation and enhanced skills

- Better general strategies

- More effective response to stress

Supporting Study
- "This study investigated the effects of an imagery rehearsal, relaxation, and self-talk package on the performance of a specific defensive basketball skill during competition. The intervention was clearly effective in enhancing a basketball skill during games, and social validity measures were very positive" (Kendall, Hrycaiko, Martin, Kendall, 1990, p. 157).

- "Additionally, imagery has been effectively used for rehearsing general strategies, learning sport specific skills, and facilitating effective responses to competitive scenarios and stressful emotions" (Abdin, 2010, p. 34).

Improved accuracy
- Improved technical quality
- Improved topspin and underspin
- Improved quality of performance

Supporting Studies

- "The results indicated that children who used mental imagery experienced significantly greater improvement in the accuracy and technical quality of their shots than children in comparison groups...The mental-training group was the only group to show significant increases in scores from pre- to post-intervention on all four measures (performance accuracy on top spun and under spun balls, technical ratings on top spun and under spun balls)...The improvement experienced by the mental training group, compared to the other two groups, appears to have been most striking in the quality of performance". Although this study involves table tennis players, I believe the principles are useful to us tennis players. It is also worth noting their imagery technique. First, they use imagery copying similar motor patterns from their preferred best world player, then imagining themselves perfectly executing the task 100 to 150 times. The authors also conclude with this: "We feel that the use of mental imagery, and mental training in general, may be particularly promising for children; it offers a means of learning skills faster and more easily". (Zhang, L., Qi-Wei, M., Orlick, T., & Zitzelsberger, L., 1992, pp. 230, 238, 239, and 240).

Evidence supporting imagery use

In conclusion, the best athletes, the elite ones, use imagery more frequently and are better at using imagery. Elite gymnasts used imagery in various forms (internal, external kinesthetic, and even auditory), and their use of imagery was more elaborate, controlled, and vivid than the unsuccessful athletes (Calmels, D'Arripe, Rournier, & Soulard, 2003). "In an unpublished report to United States Olympic Committee, Jowdy and Durtschi (1989) found that 90% of athletes and 94% of coaches surveyed at the Olympic Training Center in Colorado Springs used imagery". This was quoted in Bleecker, A (2012, p, 15). "Some 99% of athletes in this sample reported using mental imagery as a preparation strategy. On average, athletes estimated that during training they did preplanned systematic performance imagery at least once a day, 4 days per week, for about 12 minutes each time. In the last few hours at the Olympic site some reported doing this kind of imagery for 2 to 3 hours". This was a 1984 study of 235 Canadian Olympic athletes. (Orlick & Partington, 1988, p. 127)

Coaches also emphasize and utilize this mental skill, indicating its importance. In fact, many coaches feel the use of Imagery is perhaps the MOST IMPORTANT technique. Hall and

Rodgers (1989) had coaches at a coaching workshop complete a questionnaire to address the coaches' use of mental training in their lessons. They reported the coaches used imagery most often and considered it the most useful, compared to other mental skill techniques when training athletes.

All these imagery studies provide keys to Better Tennis! But let us take it further, now let us note studies specify to tennis (see next chapter)

Notes

- All the above studies apply to a variety of sports, including golf, basketball, skiing, table tennis, gymnastics, etc. Nevertheless, the principles are the same.

Chapter 32: Imagery Specific to Tennis

As I mentioned in the previous chapter, the results above are from research; they are conclusions. However, they are from a variety of sports, not just tennis. Now, let's look at the research, and what one can find in articles that are specific to tennis. Those articles indicate that practicing imagery results in...

- Better net volleys with an increase in percentage of points won at net
- Improved focus
- Improved split-second decision making
- Reduced anxiety and increased confidence
- Greater mental preparation and readiness for points and for an entire match, including being more calm and relaxed
- Reduction in time needed for warming up
- Improved performance and motor skills related to improved learning of new skills and techniques, as well as refining existing skills
- Improved serve – faster and more consistent with improved precision and accuracy, even for advanced players
- Improved service return – both accuracy and consistency
- More points won
- Improved strategies

Also, note that in some of the studies, the differences (or improvements), while significant, were small, but as noted in the chapter "A Little Goes a Long Ways" these small increments of improvement all add up and make for meaningful differences. Statistical probability moves in your favor!

Again, as in the last chapter, and to emphasize the importance and effectiveness of Imagery, I shall quote directly from the article itself.

Enhance motor skill, improve focus...

- "It can also enhance your ability to perform motor skills in competition by improving focus; helping you make plans and develop strategies; and programming your body to execute tennis shots". Athletes use imagery "to help them get the proper mindset for optimal performance" (Cohn, 2008, para. 1 and 5).

Fewer double faults, better net volleys...

- Results revealed a decrease in double fault percentage as well as an increase in the number of points won at net (Mamassis & Doganis, 2004).

111

Improved serve accuracy, precision, and consistency

- "The main results show that four mental repetitions performed in the service position help improve the precision score of the serve and that using visual imagery in the service position improves consistency in the serve … This study confirms the fact that imagery contributes to improving the precision and consistency of the serve in tennis" (Desliens, Guillot, & Rogowski, 2011, p. 10). (I want to emphasize that this was a study using advanced players, and they used the imagery while in the server position).
- "Results revealed that participants in both the imagery and self-instruction conditions served significantly more accurately than those in the control condition". The instruction was to "Imagine the whole serve, from beginning to end, including seeing the ball go into the target zone. Imagine what you would see, how you would move, and what you would feel". The difference was about 19% higher than the control group. This was a study involving about 115 participants in a serving competition (Malouff, McGee, Halford, & Rooke, 2008, p. 267 264, and 267). Note these instructions were relatively simple. A large set of instructions could be counter-productive.
- "The Imagery group had improved their performance over that of the Control Group for the serve" (Coelho, De Campos, Da Silver, Okazaki, & Keller, 2007, p. 465).

Performance improvement and self-confidence

- The result was that "All the participants of the mental training program exhibited greater performance. … None of the athletes who formed the non-mental training program group showed performance improvement. … Self-confidence was the one that showed the greatest difference between the two groups" (Mamassis & Doganis, 2004, pp. 132 and 133).
- "The intensity of self-confidence, as well as the overall tennis performance, were greater for all the participants of the Mental Training Program" (Mamassis & Doganis, 2004, p. 118).

Rehearse new skills, as well as your existing skills…

- Visual imagery "is used for rehearsing new skills, practicing and refining existing skills, preparing for particular points, and readying for an entire match. Studies have shown imagery to be helpful in a variety of ways such as reducing warm-up decrement, lowering anxiety, and increasing self-confidence" (Murray, 1995, para. 3).

Very significant studies on imagery

There were three studies that I really liked and felt were relevant. The importance of these three studies is that they demonstrate the significant impact that the use of Imagery can contribute to your tennis game. I am so appreciative of the publishers and the authors for allowing me to go into detail. It practically amounts to a public service announcement to the tennis world. I am hopeful that this gives you, the reader, the information that you need to incorporate the use of Imagery to achieve your goals for Better Tennis!

The first study is "Improving Serving Speed in Young Tennis Players". I would like to strongly and personally thank the International Tennis Federation (ITF) for their permission to allow my detailed summary of the excellent study by George Mamassis. I believe this will help many tennis players. (I will also note that George Mamassis has published several studies and articles related to tennis. The ITF and Dr. Mamassis have moved tennis forward. I hope they get more of the credit they deserve).

From George Mamassis 2005 – "Improving Serving Speed in Young Tennis Players". This is published in ITF (International Tennis Federation) Coaching and Sport Science Review, Issue 35, pp. 3-4 April 2005. This is a great study. It shows that imagery is an effective way to increase serving speed in young tennis players. Here are the details of the study:

There were 48 players ages 8-12 years of age. They all had 2 to 4 years of tennis experience. They were randomly placed in 5 groups. All groups practiced with a certified coach 3 times per week for 90 minutes per practice. The program lasted for 8 consecutive weeks. One week before the initiation and one week after the end of the intervention program, all participants were measured on their serve speed using a radar gun, imagery ability, and bench press strength. On serve speed, the mean speed of 6 serves that landed into the service box were taken into account.

Description of the 5 groups:

- **The Mental Training and Serve Practice group** (MTSP) took part in a mental training program prior to their tennis practice. Specifically, the participants of this group watched a video tape with a 14-year-old elite tennis player (whose service technique was rated as perfect by 3 expert tennis coaches) serving 9 serves, the first two at normal speed, the next 2 at half speed, the next one frame-by-frame having an expert coach emphasize 5 technical elements of a correct serve, the next 2 at half-speed, and finally the last 2 at normal speed. Then the participants closed their eyes, focused on their breathing for 30 seconds, and they tried to visualize themselves executing their serves as they saw in the video tape (2 minutes). Finally, they rated the quality of their imagery and went to the court where they also executed 30 serves. This group had the largest increase in speed – almost 5 mph.
- The Serve Practice and Strength Training group (SPST) participants followed the Serve Practice (SP) group training regimen but, after their tennis practice, they were involved in strength training (3 sets of bench press at 50%, 75%, & 100% of 10 RM). This group increased service speed to just over 3 mph.
- The Mental Training, Serve Practice and Strength Training group (MTSPST) followed a combination of the MTSP and SPST training regiments. This group also increased service speed to just over 3 mph.

- The Serve Practice group (SP) participants executed 30 serves per practice under supervision of traditional coach who made corrections (traditional way). This group increase service speed by about 2.75 mph
- The Control group (C) participated in tennis practices without practicing their serve. The Control group increased service speed a little over 1 mph.

Bottom line: The MTSP group increased their serve speed even more than the group that focused on strength training and serve practice, and included almost double the traditional serve practice routine we all do.

Results show mental imagery is an effective way to increase serving speed in young tennis players. Given that the players of the muscle training standard practice did not participate in strength training, this increase was obviously due to the improvement of their serving technique. Also, all three tennis coaches agreed that on average, the participants of the imagery group improved their technique much more than the other groups.

Study 2

There was another terrific study. This was titled "Motor Imagery and Tennis Serve Performance: The External Focus Efficacy" by Aymeric Guillot, Simon Desliens, Christelle Rouyer, and Isabelle Rogowski. It is from the Journal of Sports Science & Medicine, 2013 June; 12(2):332-338.

I would like to strongly and personally thank Dr. Hakan Gür and Dr. Aymeric Guillot for their permission to allow my detailed summary of this excellent article. This information will help so many of us aspiring tennis players. I will also note that Dr. Gür is Editor in Chief for the "Journal of Sports Science & Medicine" and Dr. Guillot is a noted and frequent publisher of numerous articles, many of which are related to tennis. I would also like to thank them for their kind comments and friendly support. It means a lot! I would like to add that Dr. Guillot is a noted researcher and a world authority on Imagery. He also offered kind words to me when I wrote him. Thanks!

This study is wonderful! It focuses on imagery using the serve, but the results also show that Mental Imagery substantially improves the probability to win more points and to win more games.

Details of the Motor Imagery and Tennis Serve Performance study:

"There were 12 high level young tennis players…They were considered national level tennis players and were therefore the best players for their age category". The study was 16 weeks long using a test and retest procedure.

"Players were instructed to mentally focus on ball trajectory and visualize the space above the net where the serve can be successfully hit. This has been defined as the 'safety window' (Brechbuhl, Tièche, & Frey, 2001)…The materialization of the 'safety window' height, evolved along the 16 motor imagery sessions. During the first four sessions, the 'safety window' was marked by a carton framework fixed on the upper border of the net. During the next four sessions, the 'safety window' was materialized by balloons, attached to the upper border of the net. For sessions 9 to 12, the 'safety window' was marked by a green elastic wire spread horizontally at the upper border of the net. Finally, during the last four sessions, the 'safety window' was no [longer] materialized".

The "players mentally rehearsed the serve once before each subsequent physical practice trial. In each Motor Imagery session, 20 tennis serves were performed (both diagonals per session), with the same instructions during the testing protocol in terms of serve velocity and accuracy. A total of 20 imagined and 20 actual trials were thus performed during each session". The players were instructed to mentally focus "on ball trajectory and specifically visualized the space above the net where the serve can be successfully hit".

After mental imaginary…

- Accuracy improved from a score of 13.6 to 16 (target in deep middle part of service box and 0.5 x 0.5 meters was 5 points, 1 x 1 meter was 3 points and in the serve box was one point).
- Service percentage improved by 8% for the control working on their serve vs 12% working on their serve and also using imagery.
- Serve velocity increased 6.2%.
- Percentage of first balls in increased 6% from 54% to 60%.
- Percentage of points won after first serve in was increased by 30%, going from 30% to 40% (I really like this part!).

The main results showed a significant increase in the accuracy and velocity of the service, as well as significant improvement in first serve and points won during the match.

This shows that "mental practice resulted in an increased accuracy score combined with decreased performance variability. Players also increased the speed of their serves (Mamassis, 2005), so that they finally served faster, more accurately, and with more consistency during the ecological serve test. Interestingly, data provided further evidence of the efficacy of Motor Imagery on serve performance in a real tennis match situation, as both the percentage and the number of won points after first-ball serves significantly increased".

"These findings not only support the effectiveness of [motor imagery] on subsequent motor performance…but also promote the efficacy of adopting an external focus of attention" (that is the use of a "safety window") when using Imagery. The data suggests motor imagery substantially improves the probability to win games.

Study 3

In my extensive review related to the use of Imagery, one of the best of all the studies includes the very important topic of return of serve. I consider this an extremely important study that the

115

tennis world (pros, coaches, players) does not seem to even be aware of. This needs to change. This one study alone should immediately convince you to start using imagery, especially on the return of serve. Before I go into the details of the study, I would like to express my sincere thanks to the study's publishers, the International Journal of Sport and Exercise Psychology, for their permission to give a detailed accounting of this experiment and data. (Note, full reference is this: Robin, N., Dominique, L., Toussaint, L., Blandin, Y., Guillot, A., & Le Her, M. (2007, January). "Effect of motor imagery training on service return accuracy in tennis: The role of imagery ability". International Journal of Sport and Exercise Psychology, 5(2), 175–186. http://dx.doi.org/10.1080/1612197X.2007.9671818. Copyright © International Society of Sport Psychology, reprinted by permission of Taylor & Francis Ltd, www.tandfonline.com on behalf of International Society of Sport Psychology.)

I would also like to thank the authors for originating and detailing such an important study. The authors are Nicolas Robin, Laurent Dominique, Lucette Toussaint, Yannick Blandin, Aymeric Guillot, and Michel Le Her. Dr. Robin has been especially kind and helpful. Note also that Nicolas Robin is a previous tennis coach and current PhD Senior Lecturer in the Sport Science University of Antilles, Guadeloupe. Laurent Dominique is a Tennis Coach, PhD, in "La Reunion Island" (Indian Ocean), Tennis Cub Dionysien, Team Run Elite.

The study summary is as follows:

The participants had played tennis for more than 7 years, and trained about 15 hours a week (for more than 3 years), competing at a regional or national level. The average age was 19 years old.

Serves were performed by 3 tennis monitors, which played toward the right serve box of the receiver. The monitors always served to the same place in the service box. The serve speed ranged from about 80-105 miles per hour.

The serve returners aimed for the deuce court between the service line and the baseline. In the middle of the square, a target was indicated by a plastic red cone (diameter: 20 cm). The area surrounding the cone was divided into 46 "sub-squares" of 10 cm. Participants had to perform service return toward the target as accurately as possible. All this was video-recorded.

Before the experiment, participants completed the Movement Imagery Questionnaire (MIQ, Hall & Pongrac, 1983). It consists of 18 items which assess individual visual and proprioceptive imagery abilities. This divided the groups into "good imagers" and "poor imagers". There was also a control group.

The study was 10 weeks long. Week 1 obtained the baseline data. "Weeks 2 to 9 involved the mental and physical training: Participants were asked (during 15 sessions) to imagine 15 service returns as well as performing 15 actual trials. The 15 imagery trials were always performed before the 15 actual trials. This combination of mental and physical practice was performed 2 times per session, in order to have a total of 60 trials (2 [sessions of] 15 imagined trials and 2 sessions of 15 actual trials). During motor imagery, performed on the tennis court in front of the experimenter, good and poor imagers were required to perform internal visual imagery (imagining being inside his/her body as if they were looking with their own eyes), by focusing their attention on the ball trajectory and on the target. This [directive] was recalled by the

116

experimenter before each imagery session. After each session, athletes were required to describe the content of their mental representation, to check that they had followed the instructions… Imagery practice was performed with the receiver in 'ready position'…In the control group, the motor imagery task was replaced by a neutral task (reading a magazine) for a time equivalent to the duration of the 15 imagined trials (about 3 minutes). Week 10 [was the] post-test: 48 hours after the end of the last training session, participants were submitted to a post-test, which was similar to the pre-test", with the participant returning 15 serves as accurately as possible toward the target.

The results: Both groups (the good imagers and the poor imagers) were substantially more consistent. Also, both groups were also significantly more accurate. The authors collected data for what they termed "amplitude" (that is, long/short distance) from the target, and what they termed as "direction" (left/right) from the target. At the end of the 10 week period, the poor imagers were 34% more accurate, and the good imagers were approximately 44% more accurate. The control group had no significant improvement.

Such an excellent study! I think this proves that internal visual imagery significantly helps the service return. It also shows that "good imagers" get better results than "poor imagers". (This is a good time to re-emphasize that the more you use imagery, the better you become at being a "good imager"). Note that they practiced 10 weeks related to the visualization, which implies that we should also practice our visualization for extended periods.

Important point of emphasis: The control group that practiced 30 service returns twice per week for 8 weeks did not improve in consistency or accuracy. However, when only 12 minutes of imagery was added per week to the practice sessions, over the 8-week period, the returns were more consistent and 34 to 44% more accurate. Imagery works!

So why aren't you using Imagery?

Chapter 33: When and How To Use Imagery

"Research has indicated that imagery just prior to performance can improve actual performance…Although it is recommended that imagery be practiced to be most effective, it appears that it can be effective (at least in laboratory tasks) with little practice if performance directly follows the use of imagery" (Weinberg, 2008, p. 4).

A combination of imaging use would be optimal, say a longer version in a quiet room at night, and a shorter version when playing points on the court. The longer, more structured version would include long focused sessions of several minutes in a quiet room 3 to 4 times per week imaging everything from focus on technique to playing points. A shorter imagery version, even while standing on the court during a game, helps when playing a match.

For now, I shall focus on the shorter version involving on-court competitive play. Image the point. Here, you are the server. You are in the deuce court and you serve a spin serve to the outside edge. You feel your body going through the serve. Then visually imagine yourself going through the service motion and hitting the outside part of the service box.

But take it further. Let's face it – it is highly probable that there will be a return cross court and you will play a forehand. So do not wait for the ball to come back. Start getting set immediately after the serve with racket back, Get Set. Then imagine your second shot where it is a forehand down the line. See yourself hitting that and coming to net. Imagine going through all the elements that compose great technique. Then, knowing it is probable that they will hit a cross-court backhand. Imagine yourself putting away the volley.

Or imagine a deuce court serve up the middle. Mentally perform the service (choose between the kinesthetic or visual – whether internal or external). Next, rehearse in your own mind playing the follow-up shot, whether it be a forehand or backhand. Imagine where you plan to hit their return shot (to wherever you have determined as their weakness, or where you are trying to probe their game for weaknesses).

The point is, do not limit yourself to a single shot on your imagery rehearsal. Imagine points played out. Many of the greats have done this!

"Before I play a match
I try to carefully rehearse in my mind
what is likely to happen
and how I will react in certain situations.
I visualize myself playing typical points based on my opponent's style of play.
I see myself hitting crisp, deep shots from the baseline
and coming to the net if I get a weak return.
This helps me mentally prepare for a match,
and I feel like I've already played the match before I even walk on the court"
Chris Evert
(as quoted by Weinberg 1988, p. 99)

In tennis, there are likely probabilities to where your opponent will hit the next shot. So prepare yourself early – Get Set! Plan your next shot in your mind! Get ahead of the point with the use of the imagery. Strategize it to where they are likely to hit their return to your strength, so you can hit the next shot to their weakness.

You enter the match more fully prepared. You step onto the court. Then play begins. The point is played out. You have already rehearsed the Get Set, the Head Turn, smoothly striking the Sweet Spot – all beautifully performing the "perfect" stroke. You then follow on through on the stroke, and go on to finish the point. Score: 15 to love.

Chapter 34: How To "Get It Done" For Imagery

General

Imagery is effective. It does not matter if you are just starting or have played for years. The better you can sync up your imagery with real life, the better your experience. The better your quality and use of imagery, the more your strokes and match play will improve. A well visualized stroke is a quality image. It is more vivid. It is more real. It translates to Better Tennis in real matches.

It is vitally important to always be rehearing the perfect techniques. Technique is everything! With visualization, you are trying to model the perfect stroke. So practice. Imaging ability improves with practice. You will develop higher quality, more vivid images. Higher quality imagers show more improvement than low quality imagers.

Imagery, even if not practiced at home, helps if you use it immediately before the point. However, those who had best results practiced imagery for several weeks.

Start Here

Google "Ultimate Slow Motion Compilation". Then select the player you want to emulate and the stroke you are trying to learn. Some of the players are Federer, Djokovic, Nadal, Murray, Dimitrov, and Serena Willams (I wish they had more compilations of the top women players). There are other slow-motion compilations, but I particularly like the "Ultimate Slow Motion Compilation" (provided by Essential Tennis). Find an ideal model player hitting the stroke you want.

Now watch the video of the players and strokes you wish to emulate – the shots you want to replicate. It should not necessarily be the best forehand, backhand, or volley in the world. Instead choose someone whose style is most like yours, whether male or female. The important thing is that stroke. We all love to watch Rafa Nadal, but few of us could ever do physically what he does to generate his strokes.

So who do you choose? That's a tough decision! Watch several YouTube videos of pros hitting forehands (for example). Now, narrow it down to your 2 or 3 favorites. Watch the videos once in the morning and before you go to bed. After a few days, watch the video immediately before your next practice against the ball machine. Copy the movements of each of your favorites. See what works. Then, of the 3 players you are copying, decide which one feels the most comfortable. Decide which one is closest to YOUR style. Decide which professional player you can realistically model your own game after. Choose that one.

Now using that one player, continue to watch that video first thing in the morning, and last thing before you go to bed (if you can only do this once per day, then the viewing before bedtime is most important). Do this at least several times per week.

Remember to study the video. Note the angle of the racket as the pros reach their Get Set position. Note their footwork. Note how they set their feet. See the angle of each foot as they prepare to start their stroke. See how the weight shifts as they go through their stroke. See how they pull their arm and shoulder back to the Get Set position. See how both arms move. See how it changes as they go through their stroke. Study the video.

Burn the image into your brain. Then replay using your imagery. First start in your home. Find a quiet place with no distractions. Then close your eyes. Start deep breathing. Try all three methods:

- **Internal visual** – Visualize yourself hitting the shot you have been working on. Visualize it as if seeing it through your own eyes. See your arms go back as you Get Set just before the ball crosses the net. You see the ball coming toward you as you focus on the small ½ inch part of the ball – the part you want to hit. You see the blur of the court as you do the Head Turn. You visualize, actually seeing, the moment where the ball just seems to hang in space, as you look directly at the ball and see yourself striking the Sweet Spot of the racket and the part of the ball you want to hit. You watch yourself going through the middle part of the stroke, your head staying motionless (the Federer pause) as you follow through. Repeat.
- **External visual** – Again, visualize yourself hitting the same shot you have been working on. Visualize it as if watching a movie. See yourself Get Set. Note the angle of your feet. Visualize your upper body starting with a fluid, smooth movement. You watch yourself hitting the middle part of the stroke after you do your Head Turn, and as the ball perfectly strikes the Sweet Spot of the racket. You observe your body follow through and complete the stroke. Repeat.
- **Kinesthetic** – You have watched the video of your favorite player (the one you most identify with) hitting the shot you are working on. Now feel your body as you mimic their movements. Feel your body as you Get Set. Sense your feet and legs as they get ready. Feel your arms as you take the racket back to the Get Set. You feel yourself swing the racket. You feel your Head Turn as you intentionally prepare to hit. You experience (in your mind) feeling your body sensations as you start a smooth stroke and strike the ball perfectly on the Sweet Spot, observing and controlling the middle part of the stroke. You feel the change in the position of your legs, shoulders, and arms as you follow through. Repeat.

Now do the chosen stroke in very slow motion – like a ninja training for the martial arts. You know – the Tai Chi stroke. You want to create the perfect stroke. Break the parts of the stroke into 10 individual parts – like still photos of one continuous movement. Use a metronome. Use one beat for each individual part of the stroke. Do this 10 times, gradually increasing the speed of the stroke. Do this at least 4 times per week then for 3 weeks. (As you know, muscle memory takes up to 3 weeks to fully establish itself).

Your goal is perfection

Focused practice makes for Better Tennis. Evans, Jones, & Mullen (2004) report "imagery requires organized, repetitive practice for it to have the desired effect on performance. Research has shown systemic practice effectively increased imagery ability" (Abdin, 2010, p. 24). This is a proven fact for imagery too. With observing the "perfect stroke" from one of the greats, and then repeatedly trying to reproduce it, you can achieve perfect technique. To paraphrase the quote in Chapter 1:

It is not how much you visualize,
but how well you visualize.

This is key to achieve effectiveness in improving your game.

Imagine all this for 5 minutes before you go to bed. Imagine this before you start practice. Imagine this as you stand on the court and prepare yourself for the next shot. Rehearse your imagery in slow motion time, and then speed it up. Then do your Tai chi strokes. Finish with real-time tempo, as that is what you will experience during the match. Imagery using real-life speeds best approximates the point you play, so practice it. The better the correlation of your imagery with real practice points, the better the results. It is more effective!

You should go through this exercise at least for 3 to 4 times per week for the next month. For imagery to be effective, it has to be practiced. It also needs to be quality imagery. Focus and concentrate on the imagery. We all have a certain amount of innate ability for imagery, some more than others, but to be really effective, practice is necessary. Like muscle memory, practice imagery on a frequent basis in a concentrated period of time. The imagery is a learned skill to be polished and honed to improve effectiveness.

It may not seem comfortable at first, but you will become more comfortable with repeated use of imagery. Remember, the more realistic the imagery, the more likely the brain translates the imagery to real life points and matches.

Anticipation skills and working on problem areas

Use imagery to work on your anticipation skills, and for shot-to-shot play as you prepare for the upcoming match. Rehearse for the upcoming point play. As noted previously, mental rehearsal using imagery has a good outcome if used immediately before the point. You rehearsed this in your room last night. Now rehearse it again just before the point.

Use imagery to work on problem areas. Let us say you are having difficulty closing a game, whether to hold service or break service. So practice imagery in anticipation of this occurring in future matches. Imagine your calm self as you return a serve. Feel the calmness within yourself. You are preparing mentally for your opponent's serve as you stand in the add court. You see the ball come to your backhand. You hit a well-paced shot wide to the opponent's add court. You have practiced this shot against the ball machine. You can now easily hit it 20 times in a row.

You are confident. Before your opponent even returns the ball, you prepare to hit your favorite shot – your forehand. You scoot back toward the add side. Now the odds of you getting a hit with your forehand are increased. You Get Set even before your opponent returns the ball. You are SO ready! Now you see the ball come back to the middle of the court and you hit a nicely paced deep shot to the corner of the deuce court. You win the point as they hit a forced error.

Now practice with your imagery as your opponent serves, not to your backhand, but to your forehand. You play out the rest of the point in your head. You have rehearsed the scenario at home sitting quietly in your room. Perhaps you have watched a similar point from a Wimbledon match. You have rehearsed the point again as you stand ready to receive the serve. Visualize this situation over and over. Rehearse again and again at home, and then especially before your opponent serves.

Notes

- **Serves** – You know from studies specific to tennis that imagery works well. The evidence is especially good related to tennis servers. So practice serving using imagery, both visual and kinesthetic. Try the concept of the safety window as described in the Dr. Guillot study. To serve precisely, think about hitting through the safety window at the net.
- **Videos** – You can improve your imagery by videotaping yourself. There are studies to support this. The video-taping syncs up your visual imagery with real life. The better you can sync up your imagery with real life, the better your experience. The better your quality and use of imagery, the more your strokes and match play will improve. You may be surprised (in a bad way) how poorly your real-life form stacks up against your imagined form as recorded on video. But this enables you to fix the differences. These days it is easy to get your phone or tablet to video tape yourself. Just be sure to get a good tripod.
- Now, just like in the "How To" chapter on muscle memory, make a Commitment Contract with yourself related to your plan to utilize imagery.

Section III: Miscellaneous

Highly Recommended Reading

Daniel Coyle – *"The Talent Code"*

I recommend reading Daniel Coyle's book, "The Talent Code", immediately after you finish this book. I think it is the perfect companion to my book. It has a lot of good information on deliberate practice. It is a great read: Enjoyable, to the point, useful, and fascinating! It will reinforce much of this. As you know, my principles and applications were totally based on my personal experience, common sense, and science. I also utilized my knowledge of the human body, neuroplasticity, rehab, etc. I made up these so called "Laws". I then attempted to extrapolate them – to take them to natural conclusions – in hopes of Better Tennis. The "Talent Code" is just the opposite. Many of his principles and conclusions are founded on field work and insightful observations, while mine were primarily theoretical (then researched to find supporting data). Yet we frequently come to the same conclusions. His book strongly reinforced what I believe. I highly recommend it in this context (understanding principles of muscle memory and how to improve one's tennis game).

Geoff Colvin – *"Talent is Overrated"*

This is another great read! Geoff Colvin's book, "Talent is Overrated", is filled with extremely important and useful information. It is very well researched and enjoyable. It too has a detailed insightful discussion of deliberate practice. You will learn so much! As above, although it has different approach from my book, it comes to many similar conclusions.

Grant Grinnell – *"Tennis Strategy: How to Beat Any Style Player"*

Grant Grinnell gives very clear succinct advice on how to play any style player in singles or doubles. There is also a section on "Mental Toughness" that is excellent. He is obviously very intelligent and observant. His summaries have a great deal of wisdom. This book should always be in your tennis bag. His book "Tennis Strategy: How to Beat Any Style Player" was reviewed 39 times (on 02/14/17) and is rated with 95% approval – for 4 and 5 stars. I am not sure I have seen a rating this good anywhere. Obviously, others think this is an outstanding book.

James Clear's weekly column

James Clear is amazing. He writes a weekly column (jamesclear.com) filled with clarity and useful information on so many subjects. His writing is outstanding on habit formation, behavioral psychology, and performance improvement. Per his web site, he studies "successful people across a wide range of disciplines – entrepreneurs, artists, athletes, and more – to uncover the habits and routines that make these people the best at what they do". Then, he shares what he learns in a free email newsletter. You probably noticed I quoted him several times. He writes well, and does a really nice job researching his content. His points are practical and applicable.

His observations and advice really help. This is not the type of column or newsletter that I usually care much about, but this one seems different. I really like it, and I think you will too!

Coach Casey Curtis

Coach Casey Curtis is at the Curtis Tennis Academy. He is recognized as one of the top developmental coaches in North America. He coached Milos Raonic for 9 years (age 8-17) during his key developmental stages. He also has coached several Canadian National Champions. The Web site is also impressive with some good information, including some good articles. He writes well. The material excellent and informative. I will visit regularly for more information and articles. http://www.curtistennis.com/federer-baryshnikov-perfection-is-no-accident.html

Florian Meier – on-line tennis instruction

http://www.onlinetennisinstruction.com

Florian's on-line video analysis and presentations are great! Some of his products includes detailed analysis of video images that you send in. He is a cool guy, and I believe he really cares and wants you to get better. He has helped my game! His video instructions are extremely well thought out. He relies on the scientific method. The videos sequentially and logically form a step-wise method for stroke progression. One component builds on the next. He strongly emphasizes the fundamentals and the biomechanical principles that will help your game. There is a wealth of really helpful information on his site. His prices seem reasonable, and some of the specials are true bargains. Once you have signed up, he also sends free instructional videos that are well worth the time. I "Highly Recommend". Go Florian!

Essential Tennis

This is a new find. First, I actually already recommended them without knowing it in this book. That reference was to the Ultimate Slow Motion Compilation video selection where some of the world's best players have extended slow-motion videos showing them hitting (I have since gone back and given Essential Tennis their due credit). It is incredible, even beautiful to watch … and it is free – courtesy of Essential Tennis. They deserve "Highly Recommended" for that alone. Then, as I explored the site more, I became even more favorably impressed. The Instructional videos are detailed, with logical progressions. They have numerous high quality youtube videos that are very well done, and free. Then, for access to even more excellent information and instruction, they have reasonable (some bargains) sign-up fees. I have since signed-up (fee paid) and spent 6-8 hours checking out the site. The conclusion – Impressive – Very Impressive. I believe it is well worth the fee!!! Another strong plus is the staff. They are enthusiastic, personable, and really seem to genuinely care. What more could you want? I "Highly Recommend"!

Ericsson, K. Anders

He is the lead author of the landmark publication, "The Role of Deliberate Practice in the Acquisition of Expert Performance" (which I recommend related to the details of deliberate practice). Dr. Ericsson also studies the development of expertise and human performance in a wide variety of domains, such as, music, medicine, chess, sports, etc. I would consider him the world's expert on deliberate practice, which studies how expert performers acquire their superior skills. He also addresses other qualities of experts to help understand and predict deliberate practice and expert performance. ("K. Anders Ericsson", 2017). He has multiple other publications and books, as well as multiple areas of research and expertise.

International Tennis Federation (ITF)

This site is awesome! The newsletter is called "ITF Coaching & Sport Science Review" (http://en.coaching.itftennis.com/coaching-sport-science-review/issue-archive.aspx or this site http://en.coaching.itftennis.com/coaching-sport-science-review/article-finder/articles-by-topic.aspx). It is "The official coaching and sport science publication of the International Tennis Federation". It has great articles and information. Examples include such titles as Carbohydrate intake for optimal performance in professional male and female players; Improving forehand performance through functional core training; Psychological factors related to choking under pressure; Men's tennis vs Women's Tennis; Principles of Adult Learning; Using apps to improve coaching: The Tennis Australia Technique App, Tactics of elite level Men's tennis (written by a coach of David Ferrer), etc. Check it out!

Tennis Warehouse University

This site is incredible!!! The amount of information is really beyond belief!!! It is about your equipment and much more. It may not mean as much to you if you do not have scientific or academic leanings, although I still think you will find it very interesting. However, if you are a scientific, formula loving, "Mythbusters" type fanatic, then this sight may be an OMG!

http://twu.tennis-warehouse.com/learning_center/index.php

http://twu.tennis-warehouse.com/learning_center/PPandspeed.php

I still feel I have not conveyed the full sense of the treasure chest of information that is on this site. I'll give a few examples to convey the full depth of information: On rackets alone, there are 24 articles/tools/experiments. For example, would you like to compare your racket to others? There are easily over 800 rackets studied and you can compare racket A to Racket B. Want to compare the power lost if you hit off center on your racket vs another racket? Again, over 800 rackets to compare. Want to see shot speed off your racket compared to another (shot speed is oncoming ball speed plus with racket tip speed)? It's there. Check vibration frequency, etc. – and all this is only for their racket division. There are 26 separate information sources related to tools/equipment/articles for strings (includes temperature and string tension, spin and impact locations, hundreds of comparisons of one string to another, etc.). Want to know about tennis balls? Then read their comparison of 26 balls from 8 brands. Some of their analytics include ball mass, ball fuzz loss on different balls, diameter size on new vs used balls, bounce height (new vs used), stiffness/deformation, etc. Hopefully you are beginning to get the picture here.

The Tennis Server

http://www.tennisserver.com is another treasure chest of knowledge. Literally hundreds of intelligently written, helpful articles covering everything from the mental aspects of the game, tennis science, equipment, tennis tips, match reports, etc. See it to believe it!

Rod Cross

See above for Tennis Warehouse. He is one of the lead guys. He personal web page is awesome! http://www.physics.usyd.edu.au/~cross/

John Wooden

His article "What a Coach Can Teach a Teacher, 1975-2004: Reflections and Reanalysis of John Wooden's Teaching Practices" is filled with incredible wisdom and insight. This article should be a Bible for any pro or coach.

mmitennis.com

Yes, this is my website. Obviously this is short for "Muscle Memory Imagery Tennis" – mmitennis.com/. This is not a finished, polished product. In fact, it is "under construction" at the time of the initial writing of this book. I hope to develop it. For now, it has a brief summary of Muscle Memory and Imagery. I plan to have an "Article of the Week" (although it may not be every week), and then archive these articles for future reference, in case someone might be interested in referring back to them. I have already written several chapters (let's call them articles now) that may be of interest. I did not include these chapters/articles in the book, as they did not quite fit into the flow and message of the book. I tried to keep the focus of the book true, rather than dilute it with some off-topic diversions.

There will also be references or links to articles (and other stuff) that would be of possible general interest to you. I also plan on having guest contributors. Who knows, but hopefully some of the academic writers I have referenced, tennis players and professionals, and even you the readers (if you are so inclined) will submit articles and provide feedback. It may be too much to dream for, but it would also be neat to have articles or comments from some of the world's top players.

I also plan to add some kind of "Comments and Discussions" section. As you know, this book came about through my knowledge, personal experience, and research. Here, I need to emphasize the personal experience. I realize that some of my suggestions may not be technically 'the best' (such as hitting the distal skyward section of the racket on ground strokes). Nevertheless, it helps me and may help you. I would like to think that many of you will try

Muscle Memory Practice, and then relate your personal experiences, or problems, with it. It would be nice to learn from each other. Think of the Website as a community 'Tennis Log'. (Remember I described the Tennis Log that you are supposes to do – see below.)

We'll see how it goes. Wish me luck! (Please)

Note:

- To repeat what I previously wrote about a Tennis Log: "By tracking your progress, you can see if you are moving ahead or not. You should figure out the effectiveness of your learning methods and strategies. Your written entries, including your personal observations and analysis, are important. What works and what doesn't? Track and learn from your log! It should be filled with helpful, insightful information".

- Email contact is: archiedan@mmitennis.com

Section IV:
Final Thoughts

Chapter 35: Personal Better Tennis Plan

Commitment Contract

I recommend that you develop a Personal Better Tennis Plan. This is my proposed model. Of course, you can make your own. First, for Muscle Memory Practice you should commit to these principles:

- Deliberate practice
- Focused practice on only one specific skill
- Repetition in a concentrated period of time
- No other types of practice occupy your practice session

Now, remember the Commitment Contract? This is the part where you do it: Create a binding agreement you sign with yourself to ensure you follow through with your intentions.

During the time period of _____ to _____,
I will commit to Muscle Memory Practice as follows:

Times per week (circle one)			Number of weeks (circle one)		
2	3	4	2	3	4
6	7	Other:	2	3	4
Repeat this _____ times within (1) (2) months					

Points of focus

These are the three key aspects of good tennis (Keystone Habits) that I recommend to focus on:

- Get Set
- Head Turn
- Sweet Spot

_____
Signature

131

Increase the odds of success

(Check those you commit to):

___ I make a public commitment by telling _____ my plan.

___ Distraction Plan: I will commit to these techniques of avoiding diversions and ensuring my Muscle Memory Practice:

_____

_____

_____

___ I will make it easy to start by (check those you commit to)

_____ Putting tennis clothes in the car.

_____ Planning for a minimum of 20 minutes on the court.

_____ Set an alarm on my phone or computer.

Other: _____

___ I will minimize my schedule (non-tennis activities) by:

_____

_____

_____

___ I will reinforce my plan by:

___ Creating a tennis log

___ Using a visual cue

___ Using these methods (_____, _____, _____) to improve

___ Have a pro review my style

___ Record a video of my stroke and review it

_____
Signature

Imagery and Tai Chi Strokes

During the time period of _____ to _____, I will commit to Imagery and Tai Chi strokes, as follows:

Times per week (circle one)			Number of weeks (circle one)		
2	3	4	2	3	4
6	7	Other:	2	3	4

Repeat this _____ times within (1) (2) months

At these times:
- ___ Evening/bedtime
- ___ Morning
- ___ Practice
- ___ Serve
- ___ During match play
- ___ Prior to anticipated upcoming shot
- ___ Volley
- ___ Forehand
- ___ Backhand
- ___ Other

Suggested 5 minute Imagery and Tai Chi strokes work out

The 5 minute visualization work out
- 1 minute of watching Ultimate Slow Motion Videos on selected stroke
- 1 minute using some type of Imagery
  - ___ Internal
  - ___ External
  - ___ Kinesthetic
- 1-minute Tai Chi strokes
- 1 minute hitting your Tai Chi strokes at the same time you watch the slow motion video.
- 1 minute of Tai Chi strokes gradually speeding up to normal speed

___ Go crazy and repeat it!

_____
Signature

Chapter: 36: Conclusion

"All Theories Are Wrong,
Some are Useful"

Historian Yuval Noah Harari writes, "Scientists usually assume that no theory is 100 per cent correct. Consequently, truth is a poor test for knowledge. The real test is utility. A theory that enables us to do new things constitutes knowledge" (Harari, 2015, p. 259). Even if most of my theories are wrong, perhaps something is useful, maybe even 2-3%.

The best ideas are the ones that help you make better choices and take wiser actions. Please review the book again (there is a lot here!), especially as related to Muscle Memory Theory and Practice – why it should work and how it is done. Break away from the traditional training and try something different. Accelerate your learning with long lasting improvements. There are no learning models or theories that are perfect. There are none that are completely true – there are only partial truths.

It matters not if all this is correct, all that really matters is how much of this is useful. If you can find just a few kernels of truth that you did not know before, then this is worthwhile. If you can find something that sets your mind off in a new and exciting direction that enables you to play Better Tennis, then that is really good. If you have discovered a new way to <u>achieve</u> a higher level, then that is really great! If I wrote something that helps the process in any way, then I am honored and feel this effort has been worthwhile. It is not about me, it is about you.

Just take a piece or two of my theory, incorporate it with your knowledge and experience, tweak it, and come up with something useful – even in a small way.

But remember what is truly important:

*"I hope everyone at the end of their playing career,
at whatever level, can say one thing I can say:
'It was fun.'
That's what means the most"*
Arthur Ashe

ENJOY!

Archie Dan

Bibliography

Abdin J. M. (2010, July). *Imagery for sport performance: A comprehensive literature review.* A research paper submitted dot the graduate school in partial fulfillment of the requirements for the degree Master of Arts, with advisor Dr. Robert Bell. Ball State University Muncie<, Indiana July 2010. 42 pages. Retrieved from http://cardinalscholar.bsu.edu/bitstream/handle/123456789/193355/AbdinJ_2010;jsessionid=63A5AA04E6FE3252F CD416EDCE542041?sequence=1

Agassi, Andre (n.d.). BrainyQuote.com. Retrieved on July 29, 2017 https://www.brainyquote.com/quotes/quotes/a/andreagass371469.html

All models are wrong. (2017, August 4). In Wikipedia, The Free Encyclopedia. Retrieved 12:55, August 5, 2017, from https://en.wikipedia.org/w/index.php?title=All_models_are_wrong&oldid=793907570

Anastasia Myskina. (2017, July 20). In Wikipedia, The Free Encyclopedia. Retrieved 21:53, August 3, 2017, from https://en.wikipedia.org/w/index.php?title=Anastasia_Myskina&oldid=791450878

Andre Agassi (2010). *Open: An Autobiography* (Vintage). London: Vintage. ISBN 0-307-38840-9.

Anna Kournikova. (2017, July 6). In Wikipedia, The Free Encyclopedia. Retrieved 21:53, August 3, 2017, from https://en.wikipedia.org/w/index.php?title=Anna_Kournikova&oldid=789284147

Austin, Howard (1974, December 1). *A Computational View of the Skill of Juggling.* A Research Report. The Artificial Intelligence Laboratory, 545 Technology Square, Cambridge, MA 02139. Sponsor: National Science Foundation, Washington, DC. Authoring Institution: Massachusetts Inst. of Tech., Cambridge. Artificial Intelligence Lab. Citable URI: http://hdl.handle.net/1721.1/6231 and https://eric.ed.gov/?id=ED128178

Bleecker, A., (2012). *Examining the self-efficacy of certified athletic trainers in their use of mental skills techniques with injured athletes.* Thesis submitted to Michigan State University in partial fulfillment of the requirements for the degree of Master of Science, Kinesiology. Retrieved from https://d.lib.msu.edu/etd/941 and Bleecker_grad.msu_0128N_11722.pdf and https://grad.msu.edu/sites/default/files/content/gradplan/GradPlanUserGuide.pdf

Bollettieri, N (2001, May 1), *Bollettieri's Tennis Handbook.* Champaign, IL: Champing. Human Kinetics.

Bowman, Bob (2012, June 16, 5:39 PM). The Mental Strategies Michael Phelps Uses to Dominate the Competition. *Business Insider.* Article by Aimee Groth where she referenced an interview by Amy Shipley. As retrieved on July 29, 2017 from http://www.businessinsider.com/the-mental-strategies-michael-phelps-uses-to-dominate-the-competition-2012-6

Brabenec, J., & Svatopluk, S., (2006, April). *The Invisible Technique: Two Seconds Decide the Result .* ITF Coaching and Sport Science Review, 38, 6-7 (ITF is International Tennis Federation. ITFTennis.com).

Brailsford, Dave. As quoted by Slater, Matt (2012, August 12). Olympics cycling: Marginal gains underpin team GB dominance. *BBC Sport.* Retrieved on July 29, 2017 from http://www.bbc.com/sport/olympics/19174302

Brashers-Krug T., Shadmehr R., & Bizzi E. (1996, July 18). Consolidation in human motor memory. *Nature, 382,* 252–255.

Brechbuhl, J., Tièche, L. & Frey, D. (2001, December 2001). Some observations on the tennis action. *ITF Coaching and Sport Science* Review. 25, 4-5. (ITF is International Tennis Federation. ITFTennis.com).

Brunt, C. (2017, August 30). *Leach's air raid spreading.* Austin American-Statesman, p. C2. Retrieved from http://digital.olivesoftware.com/Olive/ODN/AustinAmericanStatesman/Default.aspx#

Caithness, G., Osu, R., Bays, P., Chase, H., Kawato, M., Wolpert, D. M., & Flanagan, J. R.., (2004, October 6). Failure to consolidate the theory of learning for sensorimotor adaptation tasks. Journal Neuroscience, 24(40), 8662-71.

Calmels, C., D'Arripe-Longueville, F., Fournier, J., & Soulard, A. (2003, January). Competitive strategies among elite female gymnasts: An exploration of the relative influence of psychological skills training and natural learning experiences. *International Journal of Sport and Exercise Psychology*, 1(4), 327-352. doi: 10.1080/1612197X.2003.9671724

Chapman, A. R., Vicenzino, B., Blanch, P., Hodges, P. W. (2007, June 5). Leg muscle recruitment during cycling is less developed in triathletes than cyclists despite matched cycling training loads. *Experimental Brain Research*, 181(3):503-18. doi: 10.1007/s00221-007-0949-5

Chunking (psychology). (2017, May 16). In Wikipedia, The Free Encyclopedia. Retrieved 15:08, August 4, 2017, from https://en.wikipedia.org/w/index.php?title=Chunking_(psychology)&oldid=780658027

Clear, James (2015, March 31). Do more of what already works. James Clear. jamesclear.com. Retrieved on August 6, 2017 from http://jamesclear.com/checklist-solutions

Clear, James (2015, August 14). *How do experts figure out the correct things to focus on?* James Clear. jamesclear.com. Retrieved on July 29, 2017 from: http://jamesclear.com/getting-simple

Clear, James (2015, April 9). How *to stick with good habits every day by using the "Paper Clip Strategy"*. James Clear. jamesclear.com. Retrieved on July 29, 2017 from http://jamesclear.com/paper-clips

Clear, James (2015, July 17). *Warren Buffet's "20 Slot" rule: How to simplify your life and maximize your results.* James Clear. jamesclear.com. Retrieved on July 29, 2017 from http://jamesclear.com/buffett-slots

Clear, James (2016, March 7). *The proven path to doing unique and meaningful work.* James Clear. jamesclear.com. Retrieved on July 29, 2017 from http://jamesclear.com/stay-on-the-bus

Clear, James (2013, September 19). *How to stay focused when you get bored working toward your goals.* James Clear. jamesclear.com. Retrieved on July 29, 2017 from http://jamesclear.com/stay-focused

Coelho, R. W., De Campos, W., Da Silva, S. G., Okazaki, F. H. A., & Keller, B. (2007). Imagery intervention in open and closed tennis motor skill performance, *Perceptual and Motor Skills*, 105, 458-468.

Cohn, Patrick (2008, September 27). Mental imagery styles in your tennis game. *Sports Psychology for Tennis - Mental Training for Success in Tennis*. Retrieved on July 29, 2017 from website www.sportspsychologytennis.com

Colvin, G. (2008). *Talent is overrated: What really separates world-class performers from everybody else.* New York, N.Y.: Portfolio. Published by Penguin Group.

Coyle, D. (2009). *The talent code: Greatness isn't born: it's grown, here's how.* New York, New York: Published by Bantam Dell, A Division of Random House, Inc. Bantam Books.

Coyle, Daniel (2012). *The little book of talent.* New York, New York: Published by Bantam Books, A Division of Random House, Inc.

Cumming, J., Hall, C., & Shambrook, C. (2004, March). The Influence of Imagery Workshop on Athletes' Use of Imagery. *Athletic Insight The Online Journal of Sport Psychology*, 6 (1), 52-73. Retrieved on July 29, 2017 from http://www.athleticinsight.com/Vol6Iss1/InfluenceofImageryWorkshop.htm

Curtis, Casey (n.d.). *Federer & Baryshnikov, Perfection is No Accident.* Coach Curtis of the Curtis Tennis Academy. For the full article go to the link below: http://www.curtistennis.com/federer--baryshnikov-perfection-is-no-accident.html

Dave Brailsford. (2016, December 14). In Wikipedia, The Free Encyclopedia. Retrieved 15:25, August 4, 2017, from https://en.wikipedia.org/w/index.php?title=Dave_Brailsford&oldid=754748825

Declarative learning. (2016, December 25). In Wikipedia, The Free Encyclopedia. Retrieved 21:22, August 1, 2017, from https://en.wikipedia.org/w/index.php?title=Declarative_learning&oldid=756587435

Desliens, S., Guillot, A., & Rogowski, I. (2011, December). Motor imagery and serving precision: A case study, (University of Lyon, France) *ITF Coaching and Sport Science Review*, 55(19), 9-10. (ITF is International Tennis Federation. ITFTennis.com).

Dinara Safina. (2017, July 21). In Wikipedia, The Free Encyclopedia. Retrieved 21:55, August 3, 2017, from https://en.wikipedia.org/w/index.php?title=Dinara_Safina&oldid=791563843

Dmitry Tursunov. (2017, August 3). In Wikipedia, The Free Encyclopedia. Retrieved 21:58, August 3, 2017, from https://en.wikipedia.org/w/index.php?title=Dmitry_Tursunov&oldid=793739639

Driskell, J. E., Copper, C., & Moran, A., (1994, August). Does mental practice enhance performance? *Journal of Applied Psychology*, 79(4), 481-492. doi: 10.1037//0021-9010.79.4.481

Duhigg, Charles (2012). *The Power of Habit: Why We Do What We Do in Life and Business.* New York, N.Y.: Random House.

Einstein, Albert (n.d.). BrainyQuote.com. Retrieved on August 6, 2017 from https://www.brainyquote.com/quotes/quotes/a/alberteins103652.html

Elena Dementieva. (2017, July 21). In Wikipedia, The Free Encyclopedia. Retrieved 21:50, August 3, 2017, from https://en.wikipedia.org/w/index.php?title=Elena_Dementieva&oldid=791563892

Engram (neuropsychology). (2017, July 5). In Wikipedia, The Free Encyclopedia. Retrieved 21:25, August 1, 2017, from https://en.wikipedia.org/w/index.php?title=Engram_(neuropsychology)&oldid=789110645

Ericsson, K. Anders. In Wikipedia. Retrieved on 07/31/17, from https://en.wikipedia.org/wiki/K._Anders_Ericsson

Ericsson, K. A., Krampe, R. T., & Tesch-Römer, C. (1993, July). The Role of Deliberate Practice in the Acquisition of Expert Performance. *Psychological Review*, 100(3), 363-406. doi: 10.1037//0033-295X.100.3.363

Ericsson, K. A., Prietula, M. J., & Cokely, E. T. (2007, July-August). The Making of an Expert. *The Harvard Business Review*. Retrieved on July 29, 2017 from https://hbr.org/2007/07/the-making-of-an-expert

Essential Tennis. http://www.essentialtennis.com/

Federer, Roger (n.d.). AZ Quotes. Retrieved on July 29, 2017 from http://www.azquotes.com/author/4702-Roger_Federer

Federer, Roger (January 28, 2017 , Fearless Motivation, Quote #10. Retrieved on October 23, 2017 from https://fearlessmotivation.com/2017/01/28/15-roger-federer-quotes-champion/

Fisher, R., Ury, W., & Patton, B. (1991). *Getting to yes: Negotiating agreement without giving in.* New York, N.Y.: Penguin Books.

Fitzpatrick, Jasper (2010. October 1). *Use a Commitment Contract Effectively Change Habits.* lifehacker. Retrieved on July 29, 2017 from http://lifehacker.com/5653060/use-a-commitment-contract-to-effectively-change-habits

fundamental. 2017. In BusinessDictionary. Retrieved on July 29, 2017, from http://www.businessdictionary.com/definition/fundamental.html

fundamental. 2017. In dictionary.com. Retrieved on July 29, 2017, from http://www.dictionary.com/browse/fundamental?s=t

fundamental. 2017. In merriam-webster.com. Retrieved on July 29, 2017, from https://www.merriam-webster.com/dictionary/fundamental

Grinnell, Grant (2015). *Tennis strategy: How to Beat Any Style Player.* Kindle Edition. Printed by CreateSpace Print version available from www.createspace.com/ 5585101. ISBN-13: 978-1514729717 (Print). ISBN-10: 1514729717 (Print). (Kindle Locations 23-24). He has a web site at www.grantgrinnelltennis.com

Guillot, A., Desliens, S., Rouyer, C., & Rogowski, I., (2013, June). Motor imagery and tennis serve performance: The external focus efficacy. *Journal of Sports Science and Medicine,* 12, 332-338.

Guillot, A., Genevois, C., Desliens, S., Saieb, S.,, & Rogowski, I. (2012). Motor imagery and 'Placebo-racket effects' in tennis serve performance. *Psychology of Sport and Exercise,* 13, 533-540.

Gwynne, S. C. (2009, September). Mike Leach is thinking . . .. *Texas Monthly.* Retrieved on July 31, 2017 from http://www.texasmonthly.com/articles/mike-leach-is-thinking/

Habituation. (2017, May 18). In Wikipedia, The Free Encyclopedia. Retrieved 21:49, August 1, 2017, from https://en.wikipedia.org/w/index.php?title=Habituation&oldid=781007173

Hall, C., & Pongrac, J. (1983). Movement Imagery Questionnaire. London, Ontario: University of Western Ontario.

Harari, Yuval Noah (2015). *Sapiens: A Brief History of Humankind*. New York, NY. HarperCollins. Kindle Edition.

Hardy, L., & Callow, N. (1999). Efficacy of external and internal visual imagery perspectives for the enhancement of performance on tasks in which form is important. *Journal of Sport and Exercise Psychology*, 21, 95-112. Human Kinetics Publishers, Inc.

Hebbian theory. (2017, May 31). In Wikipedia, The Free Encyclopedia. Retrieved 21:55, August 1, 2017, from https://en.wikipedia.org/w/index.php?title=Hebbian_theory&oldid=783125434

Hill, Napoleon (2012). *Think and Grow Rich*. Vigo. First published 1938. This edition copyright Vigo Books, 2012. www.vigiobooks.com

John Wooden. (2017, July 11). In Wikipedia, The Free Encyclopedia. Retrieved 21:58, August 1, 2017, from https://en.wikipedia.org/w/index.php?title=John_Wooden&oldid=790111882

Joiner, W. M., & Smith, M. A. (2008, November). Long-term retention explained by a model of short-term learning in the adaptive control of reaching. *Journal of Neurology, 100*(5): 2948-2955.

Jonathan (2014, November 10). Baylor: 9 initial thoughts! Retrieved on July 29, 2017 from http://oubreakdown.com/baylor-my-initial-thoughts/

Jug, Sven. http://www.jayoogee.com/mytennismatches/Login.aspx

K. Anders Ericsson. (2017, June 30). In Wikipedia, The Free Encyclopedia. Retrieved 15:47, August 26, 2017, from https://en.wikipedia.org/w/index.php?title=K._Anders_Ericsson&oldid=788293441

Karni, A., Meyer, G., Jezzard, P., Adams, M. M., Turner, R., & Ungerleider, L. G. (1995, September 14). Functional MRI evidence for adult motor cortex plasticity during motor skill learning. *Nature*, 377, 155–158. doi:10.1038/377155a0

Karni, A., Meyer, G., Rey-Hipolito, C., Jezzard, P., Adams, M. M., Turner, R., & Ungerleider, L. (1998, February 3). The acquisition of skilled motor performance: Fast and slow experience-driven changes in primary motor cortex. *Proceedings of the National Academy of Sciences of the United States of America, 95(3)*, 861-868.

Karni, A., & Sagi, D. (1995, September 16). The time course of learning a visual skill. *Nature, 365*, 250-252. doi:10.1038/365250a0

Kelly, M (1999, revised 2004). *The rhythm of life*. United States of America. Copyright 1999 by Matthew Kelly. Revised copyright 2004 by Beacon Publishing Second Edition published by Simon & Schuster.

Kleim, J. A., Hogg, T. M., VandenBerg, P. M., Cooper, N. R., Bruneau, R., & Remple M. (2004, January 21). Cortical synaptogenesis and motor map reorganization occur during late, but not early, phase of motor skill learning. *The Journal of Neuroscience, 24*, 628–633. doi: https://doi.org/10.1523/JNEUROSCI.3440-03.2004

Klinzing, M. (2015, August 21). Basketball on the edge - The Kaizen approach to basketball training. *Head Start Basketball*. As retrieved on July 30, 2017 from http://www.headstartbasketball.com/basketball-on-the-edge-the-kaizen-approach-to-basketball-training/

Krakauer, J. W., & Shadmehr, R. (2006, January.) Consolidation of motor memory, *Trends in Neuroscience, 29*(1), 58-64. doi:10.1016/j.tins.2005.10.003.

labile. 2017. In In merriam-webster.com. Retrieved on July 29, 2017, from https://www.merriam-webster.com/dictionary/labile

Larisa Preobrazhenskaya (n.d). Retrieved from Coyle 2009 . *The talent code* (see above for full reference).

Laughlin, Terry (2009, January 14). Video: What 'Muscle Memory" looks like. *Total Immersion Swimming*. Retrieved on July 29, 2017 from http://www.totalimmersion.net/blog/video-what-muscle-memory-looks-like/

Laughlin, Terry (2008). Total Immersion: About Terry Laughlin. Retrieved on July 29, 2017 from https://www.totalimmersion.net/about-terry-laughlin

Leach, Mike (2012). As quoted by David Purdum (2012, October). The Pirate Returns - Mike Leach brings his high-powered but surprisingly simple passing offense to Washington State. American Football Monthly. Retrieved on July 30, 2017 from http://www.americanfootballmonthly.com/Subaccess/articles.php?article_id=5944

139

Lee, Bruce (n.d.). BrainyQuote.com. Retrieved on July 29, 2017 from BrainyQuote.com Web site: https://www.brainyquote.com/quotes/quotes/b/brucelee413509.html

Letts, Gregg (2007). Are the Chinese coaches correct? about.com.

Liu, X., Ramirez, S., Pang, P. T., Puryear, C. B., Govindarajan, A., Deisseroth, K., & Tonegawa, S. (2012, April 19). Optogenetic stimulation of a hippocampal engram activates fear memory recall. *Nature*, 484(7394), 381–385. http://doi.org/10.1038/nature11028

Luft, A. R., & Buitrago, M. M., (2005, December). Stages of Motor Skill Learning. *Molecular Neurobiology*, 32(3): 205-216. https://doi.org/10.1385/MN:32:3:205

Macci, R. (2015, October 21). As retrieved on August 6, 2017 from https://www.youtube.com/watch?v=5MHugAF2DiQ&t=1m33s

Mahoney, M. J., & Avener, M. (1977, June). Psychology of the elite: An exploratory study. *Cognitive Therapy and Research*, 1(2), 135-141.

Malouff, J. M., McGee, J. A., Halford, H. T., & Rooke, S. E. (2008, September). Effects of pre-competitions positive imagery and self-instructions on accuracy of serving tennis. *Journal of Sport Behavior*, 31(3), 264-275.

Mamassis, George (2005, April). Improving serving speed in young tennis players. *ITF - Coaching and Sport Science Review*, 35 (3-4). (ITF is International Tennis Federation. ITFTennis.com).

Mamassis, G., & Doganis, G, (2004). The effects of a mental training program on juniors pre-competitive anxiety, self-confidence, and tennis performances. *Journal of Applied Sport Psychology*, 16(2), 118-137, doi:10.1080/10413200490437903

Maraniss, D. (1999). *When pride still mattered: A life of Vince Lombardi*. New York, NY: Simon & Schuster.

Marat Safin. (2017, August 1). In Wikipedia, The Free Encyclopedia. Retrieved 21:54, August 3, 2017, from https://en.wikipedia.org/w/index.php?title=Marat_Safin&oldid=793349571

Martin, K.A., & Hall, C. R. (1995, March). Using mental imagery to enhance intrinsic motivation. *Journal of Sport and Exercise Psychology*, 17(1), 54-69. https://doi.org/10.1123/jsep.17.1.54

Marzorati, G. (2016). *Late to the ball*. New York, NY. Simon & Schuster.

Meier, Florian (2017, April 25). How to Hit your forehand like Roger Federer. [You Tube]. Retrieved on July 29, 2017 from https://www.youtube.com/watch?v=DBfbcEdomic&list=PLsLT-K5N043fA2adEUSoiO0dLm_0b95bW&index=1

Memory. (2017, July 24). In Wikipedia, The Free Encyclopedia. Retrieved 22:26, August 1, 2017, from https://en.wikipedia.org/w/index.php?title=Memory&oldid=792125265

Michael Phelps. (2017, July 31). In Wikipedia, The Free Encyclopedia. Retrieved 13:40, August 5, 2017, from https://en.wikipedia.org/w/index.php?title=Michael_Phelps&oldid=793243681

Mikhail Youzhny. (2017, July 10). In Wikipedia, The Free Encyclopedia. Retrieved 22:00, August 3, 2017, from https://en.wikipedia.org/w/index.php?title=Mikhail_Youzhny&oldid=789996638

Milne, S., Orbell, S., & Sheeran, P. (2002, May). Combining motivational and volitional interventions to promote exercise participation: Protection motivation theory and implementation intentions. *British Journal of Health Psychology*, 7(Pt2), 163-184.

Monica Seles. (2017, August 27). In Wikipedia, The Free Encyclopedia. Retrieved 19:25, September 10, 2017, from https://en.wikipedia.org/w/index.php?title=Monica_Seles&oldid=797486655

Motor learning. (2017, May 4). In Wikipedia, The Free Encyclopedia. Retrieved 22:36, August 1, 2017, from https://en.wikipedia.org/w/index.php?title=Motor_learning&oldid=778689816

Motor Skill Consolidation. (2015, August 28). In Wikipedia, The Free Encyclopedia. Retrieved 21:11, August 3, 2017, from https://en.wikipedia.org/w/index.php?title=Motor_Skill_Consolidation&oldid=678223135

Munroe-Chandler, K., Hall, C., & Fishburne, G. (2008, December). Playing with confidence: The relationship between imagery use and self-confidence and self-efficacy in youth soccer players. *Journal of Sports Sciences, 26*, (14). doi; 10.1080/02640410802315419

Murray, John (1995, August). The Expense of Imagery in Tennis. From Tennis Warehouse - The Tennis Server - Mental Equipment. Retrieved on July 30, 2017 from http://www.tennisserver.com/mental-equipment/me_8_95.html

Muscle memory. (2017, June 12). In Wikipedia, The Free Encyclopedia. Retrieved 22:17, August 1, 2017, from https://en.wikipedia.org/w/index.php?title=Muscle_memory&oldid=785285455

Neil, R., Mellalieu, S. D., Hanton, S., (2006). Psychological Skills Usage and the Competitive Anxiety Response as a Function of Skill Level in Rugby Union. *Journal Sports Science & Medicine, 5*(3), 415–423.

Nezam, S. E., IsaZadeh, H., Hojjati, A., & Zadeh, Z. B. (2014). Comparison ability of movement imagery perspectives in elite, sub-elite, and non elite athletes. *International Research Journal of Applied and Basic Sciences, 8*(6), 712-716.

Oransky, M. (n.d.). Retrieved on August 5, 2017 from http://gainesvilletennisacademy.com/training-resources/.

Orlick, T. & Partington, J. (1988, June). Mental links to excellence. *The Sport Psychologist, 2*(2), 105-130. doi: 10.1123/tsp.2.2.105

Page, S. J., Sime, W., & Nordell, K. (1999, December). The effects of imagery on female collegiate swimmers' perceptions of anxiety. *The Sport Psychologist, 13*(4), Issue 458-469. https://doi.org/10.1123/tsp.13.4.458

Pareto analysis. (2017, August 3). In Wikipedia, The Free Encyclopedia. Retrieved 21:22, August 3, 2017, from https://en.wikipedia.org/w/index.php?title=Pareto_analysis&oldid=793773548

Pareto principle. (2017, July 31). In Wikipedia, The Free Encyclopedia. Retrieved 21:17, August 3, 2017, from https://en.wikipedia.org/w/index.php?title=Pareto_principle&oldid=793256105

Perfect is the enemy of good. (2017, July 21). In Wikipedia, The Free Encyclopedia. Retrieved 21:12, August 3, 2017, from https://en.wikipedia.org/w/index.php?title=Perfect_is_the_enemy_of_good&oldid=791607518

Plessinger, A. (2000). The effects of mental imagery on athletic performance. *The Health Psychology Home Page*, Psychology Department at Vanderbilt University. The Health Psychology Home Page is produced and maintained by David Schlundt, PhD. Retrieved on July 30, 2017 from http://healthpsych.psy.vanderbilt.edu/HealthPsych/mentalimagery.html

Practice (learning method). (2017, July 29). In Wikipedia, The Free Encyclopedia. Retrieved 21:31, August 3, 2017, from https://en.wikipedia.org/w/index.php?title=Practice_(learning_method)&oldid=792959748

Procedural memory. (2017, July 20). In Wikipedia, The Free Encyclopedia. Retrieved 22:33, August 1, 2017, from https://en.wikipedia.org/w/index.php?title=Procedural_memory&oldid=791469043

Purdum, David (2012, October). The Pirate Returns - Mike Leach brings his high-powered but surprisingly simple passing offense to Washington State. *American Football Monthly*. Retrieved on July 30, 2017 from http://www.americanfootballmonthly.com/Subaccess/articles.php?article_id=5944

Quote Investigator (n.d.). Retrieved on September 9, 2017 from https://quoteinvestigator.com/2017/03/23/same/

Rasch, B., & Born, J. (2013, April). About Sleep's Role in Memory. *Physiology Reviews, 93*(2): 681–766. doi: 10.1152/physrev.00032.20122

Rattanakoses, R., Omar-Frauzee, M. S., Geok, S. K., Abdullah, M. C., Choosakul, C., Nazaruddin, M. N., & Nordin, H. (2009, December). Evaluating the Relationship of Imagery and Self-Confidence in Female and Male Athletes. *European Journal of Social Sciences, 10*(1).

Robbins, Anthony (2014). *Money, Master the Game: 7 Simple Steps to Financial Freedom*. New York, London, Toronto, Sydney, New Delhi. Simon & Schuster.

Robin, N., Dominique, L., Toussaint, L., Blandin, Y., Guillot, A., & Le Her, M. (2007, January). Effect of motor imagery training on service return accuracy in tennis: The role of imagery ability. *International Journal of Sport and Exercise Psychology*, 5(2), 175–186. . http://dx.doi.org/10.1080/1612197X.2007.9671818. Copyright © International Society of Sport Psychology, reprinted by permission of Taylor & Francis Ltd, www.tandfonline.com on behalf of International Society of Sport Psychology.

Roddick, Andy (n.d.). Retrieved on August 6, 2017 from http://rickmacci.com

Rohn, Jim (n.d.). *The Quote of the Day Show*. Retrieved on July 30, 2017 from http://quoteofthedayshow.libsyn.com/012-jim-rohn-the-formula-for-success-is-a-few-simple-disciplines-practiced-every-day

Rotella, R. J., Gansneder, B., Ojala, D., & Billing, J. (1980). Cognitions and coping strategies of elite skiers: an exploratory study of young developing athletes. *Journal of Sport Psychology*, 2, 350-354.

Seidler, R. D (2010, January 9). Neural correlates of motor learning, transfer of learning, and learning to learn. *Exercise and Sport Sciences Reviews*, 38(1), 3-9. doi: 10.1097/JES.0b013e3181c5cce7

Shadmehr, R., & Brashers-Krug, T. (1997, January 1). Functional stages in the formation of human long-term motor memory. *The Journal of Neuroscience, 17*(1), 409-419.

Slater, Matt (2012, August 12). *Olympics cycling: Marginal gains underpin team GB dominance*. BBC Sport. http://www.bbc.com/sport/olympics/19174302. Retrieved on July 29, 2017.

Spartak Tennis Club. (2017, February 23). In Wikipedia, The Free Encyclopedia. Retrieved 21:47, August 3, 2017, from https://en.wikipedia.org/w/index.php?title=Spartak_Tennis_Club&oldid=766979761

Teixeira, L. A. (2000, August 18). Timing and force components in bilateral transfer of learning. Brain and Cognition, 44, 255-469.

Tennis Warehouse University. Retrieved on July 30, 2017 from http://twu.tennis-warehouse.com/cgi-bin/comparepower.cgi

Tennis Warehouse University. Retrieved on August 25, 2017 from http://twu.tennis-warehouse.com/learning_center/location.php

Ungerleider, S., & Golding, J. M.(1991, June 1). Mental practice among olympic athletes. *Perceptual and Motor Skills, Volume 72*, Issue 3, 1007-1017. doi: 10.2466/PMS.72.3.1007-1017

University Of Maryland, Baltimore (1997, August) 7. Motor memory: Skills slip most easily in first hours after learning. *ScienceDaily*. Retrieved on July 30, 2017 from https://www.sciencedaily.com/releases/1997/08/970806145740.htm

University of Minnesota Duluth (n.d.). Chapter 12 Transfer of learning. Retrieved on August 6, 2017 from http://www.d.umn.edu/~dmillsla/courses/motorlearning/documents/Chapter12.pdf

Vadoa, E. A., Hall, C. R., & Moritz, S. E. (1997, September). The relationship between competitive anxiety and imagery use. *Journal of Applied Psychology*. 9(2), 241-253. doi: 10.1080/10413209708406485

Vaswani, P. A., & Shadmehr, R., (2013, May 1). Decay of Motor Memories in the Absence of Error. *Journal of Neuroscience, 33*(18), 7700-7709; doi: 10.1523/JNEUROSCI.0124-13.2013

Vilfredo Pareto. (2017, July 28). In Wikipedia, The Free Encyclopedia. Retrieved 21:27, August 3, 2017, from https://en.wikipedia.org/w/index.php?title=Vilfredo_Pareto&oldid=792824740

Vince Lombardi. (2017, August 2). In Wikipedia, The Free Encyclopedia. Retrieved 22:18, August 3, 2017, from https://en.wikipedia.org/w/index.php?title=Vince_Lombardi&oldid=793586691

Visser, C. (2010, January). Deliberate practice and deep practice. *The Progress-Focused Approach*. A Blog by Coert Visser. Retrieved on July 30, 2017 from http://www.progressfocused.com/2010/01/deliberate-practice-and-deep-practice.html

Walker M. P., Brakefield T., Hobson J. A., & Stickgold R. (2003, October 9). Dissociable stages of human memory consolidation and reconsolidation. *Nature, 425*, Issue 6958, 616–620. https://doi.org/10.1038/nature01930

Weinberg, R., (1988). *The mental advantage*. Champaign, IL. Leisure Press.

Weinberg, R. (2008, January). Does imagery work? Effects on performance and mental skills. Journal of Imagery Research in Sport and Physical Activity, 3(1), Article 1. doi: 10.2202/1932-0191.1025

White, A., & Hardy, L., (1995, May). Use of different imagery perspectives on the learning and performance of different motor skills. *British Journal of Psychology*, 86(2): 169-180. doi: 10.1111/j.2044-8295.1995.tb02554.x

Williams, S. E., Cumming, J., & Balanos, G. M., (2010, June). The use of imagery to manipulate challenge and threat appraisal states in athletes. Journal of Sport & Exercise Psychology, 32(3), 339-358. doi: 10.1123/jsep.32.3.339

Wooden, John (n.d.). AZQuotes. Retrieved on August 6, 2017 from http://www.azquotes.com/quote/434872

Wooden, John. (n.d.). AZQuotes.com. Retrieved February 04, 2017, from http://www.azquotes.com/quote/823224

Wooden, John & Jamison, Steve (1997). *Wooden: A lifetime of observation and reflections on and off the court.* New York. McGraw-Hill.

Xu T., Yu X., Perlik A. J., Tobin W. F., Zweig J. A., Tennant K., et al. . (2009). Rapid formation and selective stabilization of synapses for enduring motor memories. *Nature, 462*, 915–919. doi:10.1038/nature08389

Yevgeny Kafelnikov. (2017, July 31). In Wikipedia, The Free Encyclopedia. Retrieved 21:52, August 3, 2017, from https://en.wikipedia.org/w/index.php?title=Yevgeny_Kafelnikov&oldid=793280248

Yoda (n.d.). Yoda Quotes. Retrieved on August 4, 2017 from http://www.yodaquotes.net/page/6/

Zhang, L., Qi-Wei, M., Orlick, T., & Zitzelsberger, L. (1992, September). The effect of mental imager training on performance enhancement with 7-10 year-old children. *The Sport Psychologist, 1992*, 6(3), 230-241. https://doi.org/10.1123/tsp.6.3.230

Made in the USA
Columbia, SC
13 August 2023

21581158R00080